Congressional Research Service

Informing the legislative debate since 1914

Armed Conflict in Syria: Overview and U.S. Response

Carla E. Humud, Coordinator
Analyst in Middle Eastern Affairs

Christopher M. Blanchard
Specialist in Middle Eastern Affairs

Mary Beth D. Nikitin
Specialist in Nonproliferation

May 26, 2017

Congressional Research Service

7-5700

www.crs.gov

RL33487

Summary

A deadly chemical weapons attack in Syria on April 4, 2017, and a U.S. military strike in response on April 6 returned the Syrian civil war—now in its seventh year—to the forefront of international attention. In response to the April 4 attack, some Members of Congress called for the United States to conduct a punitive military operation. These Members and some others since have praised President Trump's decision to launch a limited strike, although some also have called on the President to consult with Congress about Syria strategy. Other Members have questioned the President's authority to launch the strike in the absence of specific prior authorization from Congress. In the past, some in Congress have expressed concern about the international and domestic authorizations for such strikes, their potential unintended consequences, and the possibility of undesirable or unavoidable escalation.

Since taking office in January 2017, President Trump has stated his intention to "destroy" the Syria- and Iraq-based insurgent terrorist group known as the Islamic State (IS, also known as ISIL, ISIS, or the Arabic acronym *Da'esh*), and the President has ordered actions to "accelerate" U.S. military efforts against the group in both countries. In late March, senior U.S. officials signaled that the United States would prioritize the fight against the Islamic State and said that Syrian President Bashar al Asad's future would be determined by the Syrian people. Nevertheless, following the April 4 attack, President Trump and senior members of his Administration have spoken more critically of Asad's leadership, and it remains to be seen whether the United States will more directly seek to compel Asad's departure from power while pursuing the ongoing campaign against the Islamic State.

Since late 2015, Asad and his government have leveraged military, financial, and diplomatic support from Russia and Iran to improve and consolidate their position relative to the range of antigovernment insurgents arrayed against them. These insurgents include members of the Islamic State, Islamist and secular fighters, and Al Qaeda-linked networks. While Islamic State forces have lost territory to the Syrian government, to Turkey-backed Syrian opposition groups, and to U.S.-backed Syrian Kurdish and Arab fighters since early 2016, they remain capable and dangerous. The IS "capital" at Raqqah has been isolated, but large areas of central and eastern Syria remain under the group's control. The presence and activities of Russian military forces and Iranian personnel in Syria create complications for U.S. officials and military planners, and raise the prospect of inadvertent confrontation with possible regional or global implications.

Since March 2011, the conflict has driven more than 5 million Syrians into neighboring countries as refugees (out of a total pre-war population of more than 22 million). More than 6.3 million other Syrians are internally displaced and are among more than 13.5 million Syrians in need of humanitarian assistance. The United States is the largest donor of humanitarian assistance to the Syria crisis (which includes assistance to neighboring countries hosting refugees), and since FY2012 has allocated more than $6.5 billion to meet humanitarian needs. In addition, the United States has allocated more than $500 million to date for bilateral assistance programs in Syria, including the provision of nonlethal equipment to select opposition groups. President Trump has requested $191.5 million in FY2018 funding for such assistance and $500 million in FY2018 defense funds to train and equip anti-IS forces in Syria.

U.S. officials and Members of Congress continue to debate how best to pursue U.S. regional security and counterterrorism goals in Syria without inadvertently strengthening U.S. adversaries or alienating U.S. partners. The Trump Administration and Members of the 115th Congress—like their predecessors—face challenges inherent to the simultaneous pursuit of U.S. nonproliferation, counterterrorism, civilian protection, and stabilization goals in a complex, evolving conflict.

Contents

Overview 1

   April 2017 Chemical Weapons Attack and U.S. Response 2

      Presidential Authority to Strike Syria Under U.S. Law 4

      Sanctions on the Syrian Scientific Studies and Research Center.. 6

Issues for Congress and Select Pending Legislation 6

   Select Proposed Syria-Related Legislation 7

Conflict Synopsis 9

   Russia's Military Intervention 11

Recent Developments 12

   Military... 12

      SDF Operations to Isolate Raqqah.. 12

      Ongoing U.S. Presence in Manbij.. 16

      Turkish-Supported Operations in Syria 16

      Syria-Iraq-Jordan Tri-border Area 18

   Political Negotiations... 19

      The Geneva Process... 19

      The Astana Process 20

   Humanitarian Situation 22

      International Humanitarian Funding... 23

      U.S. Humanitarian Assistance... 24

U.S. Policy and Assistance 24

   Perceived Threats and Challenges for Policymakers 24

   U.S. Strategy and Policy 25

   U.S. Assistance to Syrians and the Syrian Opposition 27

      Nonlethal Assistance to Armed Syrian Opposition Elements.. 29

      Syria Train and Equip Program... 30

      Related Appropriations and Authorities... 31

      Other Reported U.S. Assistance.. 33

   Chemical Weapons and Disarmament... 35

Outlook... 39

Figures

Figure 1. Syria: Areas of Influence... 5

Figure 2. Raqqah Operations... 15

Figure 3. Syria-Turkey Border 17

Tables

Table 1. Syria Train and Equip Program: Appropriations Actions and Requests 32

Contacts

Author Contact Information 40

Overview

After six years of conflict, the challenges posed to U.S. national security by the situation in Syria have multiplied and evolved. Initial political unrest and the Syrian government's violent response fueled U.S. concerns about Syria's stability and civilian protection in the midst of the 2011 "Arab Spring." The country's subsequent descent into brutal war created a multifaceted regional security crisis, marked by the mass displacement of civilians, the emergence and empowerment of violent armed Islamist extremist groups, gross human rights abuses and war crimes, the use of chemical weapons, the proliferation of arms, and the covert and overt intervention of outside actors. Over time, U.S. policymakers have appeared to feel both compelled to respond to these interlocking crises and cautious in considering potentially risky options for doing so, such as the commitment of military combat forces or the provision of lethal assistance to Syrian combatants. The Obama Administration supported various partner forces in Syria, while calling for Asad's ouster through a negotiated transition.

Russia's forceful entrance into the conflict in 2015 bolstered flagging Syrian government forces, but has yet to enable President Bashar al Asad to reassert control over all of Syria. Government forces and their foreign allies (chiefly Russia, Iran, Lebanese Hezbollah, and Iraqi Shia militia groups) have gained at the expense of their various insurgent adversaries since late 2015, but armed opposition groups continue to control territory and durable political and military solutions remain elusive. Progress has been made by various parties in reducing the amount of territory held by the Islamic State, but competition and discord among local, regional, and extraregional actors continues to create complications for U.S. officials. As of 2017, principal U.S. concerns focus on combatting the Islamic State (IS, also known as ISIS/ISIL or by the Arabic acronym *Da'esh*) and other Syria-based extremists, while seeking a resolution to the underlying conflict.

In Congress, Members have weighed the relative risks and rewards of various proposed courses of action against the Islamic State and the Asad government while conducting oversight of U.S. assistance programs and military operations. To date, the United States has directed more than $6.5 billion toward Syria-related humanitarian assistance, and Congress has appropriated billions more to support security and stabilization initiatives in Syria and in neighboring countries. The Defense Department has not disaggregated the costs of military operations in Syria from the overall cost of Operation Inherent Resolve, which has reached over $11.7 billion. As of late 2016, Congress had approved the use of more than $1.3 billion to train and equip vetted Syrians as part of a specially authorized program in place since late 2014. Congress also has debated proposals to authorize or restrict the use of military force against the Islamic State and in response to Syrian government chemical weapons attacks, but has not enacted any Syria-specific force authorizations.

An April 2017 chemical weapons attack in Syria and resulting U.S. missile strikes rekindled debates in Congress about Syria policy, and these debates may intensify as the Trump Administration considers its options and further articulates its goals and strategy. Operations against the Islamic State are focused on the isolation and recapture of the city of Raqqah. After Raqqah, U.S. military officials and local partners may move against IS strongholds in the eastern Euphrates River valley, including areas adjacent to the Iraqi border. The 115th Congress is considering FY2018 appropriations and authorization legislation related to Syria, and may engage in renewed debate about overall U.S. strategy while considering the Trump Administration's FY2018 funding requests.

Immediate debates and developments notwithstanding, the degree of devastation and displacement already wrought by the conflict in Syria is overwhelming and may take Syrians and their neighbors decades to overcome. This context and the ongoing intersection in Syria of multiple U.S. national security interests suggest that Congress may face tough choices about U.S. Syria policy and related U.S. relief and security assistance programs for years to come.

April 2017 Chemical Weapons Attack and U.S. Response

On April 4, 2017, Syrian aircraft operating in rebel-held Idlib province conducted several airstrikes using what U.S. officials assessed to be a chemical nerve agent.[1] Initial reports suggest that the strikes killed roughly 80 to 100 people in the town of Khan Sheikhoun (see map, **Figure 1**), including children, and affected several hundred others.[2] While Syrian and Russian officials blamed the deaths on rebel fighters, claiming that Syrian airstrikes hit a warehouse containing rebel-manufactured chemical weapons, U.S. officials attributed the use of chemical weapons to the Syrian government.

On April 6, the United States fired 59 Tomahawk missiles at Al Shayrat airfield in Homs province (see map, **Figure 1**), from which U.S. intelligence sources had concluded the Khan Sheikhoun attack was launched.[3] U.S. military officials stated that the strikes targeted Syrian aircraft and infrastructure. Speaking on April 6, President Trump said

> Tonight, I ordered a targeted military strike on the airfield in Syria from where the chemical attack was launched. It is in this vital national security interest of the United States to prevent and deter the spread and use of deadly chemical weapons. There can be no dispute that Syria used banned chemical weapons, violated its obligations under the Chemical Weapons Convention, and ignored the urging of the U.N. Security Council.

A Defense Department statement said the U.S. strike "targeted aircraft, hardened aircraft shelters, petroleum and logistical storage, ammunition supply bunkers, air defense systems, and radars" and that "the strike was intended to deter the regime from using chemical weapons again."[4] While Russia established a presence at Al Shayrat airfield in late 2015,[5] U.S. military officials stated that there were no Russian aircraft present at the time of the strikes, and said Russian facilities and personnel were not targeted.[6] U.S. military officials stated that Russian military personnel were informed prior to the attack, via an established deconfliction channel. A Defense Department assessment released on April 10 stated that the U.S. strike "resulted in the damage or destruction of fuel and ammunition sites, air defense capabilities, and 20 percent of Syria's operational aircraft."[7] Secretary Mattis later clarified that "around 20 aircraft were taken out" by the strike.[8]

The Syrian military released a statement describing the strikes against Al Shayrat as an "act of aggression," which killed six people and caused "huge material damage."[9] Syrian state media reported that some U.S. missiles struck nearby villages, killing nine civilians, including

---

[1] President Trump Statement on Syria, April 6, 2017; and, Statement from Pentagon Spokesman Capt. Jeff Davis on U.S. strike in Syria, Release No: NR-126-17, April 6, 2017.

[2] A document released by the White House cites local sources estimating 50 to 100 fatalities. The French government's declassified assessment on the attack estimates that more than 80 people were killed.

[3] Ibid.

[4] Statement from Pentagon Spokesman Capt. Jeff Davis on U.S. strike in Syria, Release No: NR-126-17, April 6, 2017.

[5] "Report: Russia Is Building a Second Military Airbase in Syria," *Business Insider*, December 3, 2015.

[6] "Dozens of U.S. Missiles Hit Air Base in Syria," *New York Times*, April 6, 2017.

[7] Statement by Secretary of Defense Jim Mattis on the U.S. Military Response to the Syrian Government's Use of Chemical Weapons, April 10, 2017.

[8] Press Conference by Secretary Mattis and Gen. Votel in the Pentagon Briefing Room, April 11, 2017.

[9] "Army Command: US Missile Attack Violates Int'l Laws, Makes the US a Partner of Terrorist Organizations," *Syrian Arab News Agency*, April 7, 2017.

children.[10] CRS cannot verify these reports. A spokesperson for Russian President Vladimir Putin said that Putin considered the attacks to be an act of aggression against a sovereign state in violation of the norms of international law, and said the U.S. strike "impairs" U.S.-Russian relations.[11] U.S. military officials stated that Russia had notified them of its intent to suspend communications via the deconfliction channel, which was established to help the two states avoid conflict between their respective forces operating in Syria. A Russian spokesperson told reporters that Russia would keep military channels of communication open with the United States, but would not provide any information through them.[12]

President Trump did not seek congressional authorization prior to ordering the attack. Reports suggest that some Members of Congress were notified as the strikes were underway. While some Members praised the U.S. strikes, several of these have also called upon the Administration to consult Congress on U.S. strategy in Syria and on any more expansive or persistent military operations in Syria beyond ongoing counterterrorism missions. Some Members have questioned whether the strike had sufficient domestic or international legal justification.

It is unclear what, if any, impact the strikes had on the Syrian government's calculus or on its broader military or political strategy. The strikes have not significantly altered the pace or effectiveness of pro-regime airstrikes—the vast majority of which are conducted with conventional rather than chemical weapons.[13] On April 7, a Syrian human rights organization reported that two aircraft took off from Al Shayrat and struck targets near the city of Palmyra.[14] Syrian and Russian forces have continued airstrikes against rebel-held areas, including Khan Sheikhoun.[15] In an April 13 interview, Syrian President Asad stated,

> what we and the Russians announced about a few airplanes being destroyed, most of them are the old ones, some of them were not active anyway. This is the reality, and the proof is that, since the strike, we haven't stopped attacking terrorists all over Syria. So, we didn't feel that we are really affected.[16]

It is unclear whether Syrian or Russian forces will seek to further escalate tensions by targeting U.S. military personnel or U.S.-backed local forces operating in Syria. American officials stated that U.S. military activities in Syria have been slightly adjusted to strengthen the protection of U.S. forces.[17] On May 18, coalition forces struck Syrian pro-government fighters approaching the border town of At Tanf, where U.S.-backed opposition forces are based. U.S. military officials stated that the advance posed a threat to U.S. partner forces. (See "Syria-Iraq-Jordan Tri-border Area").

U.S. decisionmakers may consider options for responding to any Russian efforts to repair Syrian military infrastructure and replace aircraft and materiel lost in the U.S. strike. Russia may also seek to further employ or strengthen its Syria-based air defense networks. If the Asad government were to use chemical weapons again, U.S. officials might face questions about whether the United States should take more punitive or disruptive measures as a deterrent, with uncertain

---

[10] "Nine Civilians Killed in US Missile Attack in Homs," *Syrian Arab News Agency*, April 7, 2017.

[11] "Putin Calls US Strikes Against Syria 'Aggression Against Sovereign Country,'" *TASS* (Russia), April 7, 2017.

[12] "Russia Notifies Intent to Suspend Communication Channel: Coalition Official," *Reuters*, April 7, 2017.

[13] "Russia's Unrelenting Attacks on Syrian Civilians," Institute for the Study of War, April 29, 2017.

[14] "Jets Launch Raids from Syria Base hit by US: Monitor," AFP, April 7, 2017.

[15] "Syria strikes: Site of chemical attack hit again," *CNN*, April 8, 2017.

[16] Transcript, Syrian President Asad interview with AFP, April 13, 2017.

[17] "U.S. bolsters protection of forces in Syria as tensions climb," *Reuters*, April 10, 2017.

implications for the viability of pro-Asad forces in the broader conflict and for U.S. relations with Russia and Iran.

Trump Administration officials reportedly have assured Members of Congress that the April 6 strikes were not the planned start of an extended military campaign against the Syrian government.[18] Speaking at the U.N. Security Council on April 7, U.S. Permanent Representative to the United Nations Ambassador Nikki Haley said

> The United States will no longer wait for Assad to use chemical weapons without any consequences. Those days are over. But now we must move to a new phase, a drive toward a political solution to this horrific conflict. We expect the Syrian regime and its allies to take the U.N. political process seriously, something they have not done up until this point. We expect Russia and Iran to hold their ally accountable and abide by the terms of the cease-fire. We expect this Council to speak loudly and forcefully when the regime or its allies undermine the political process and countless of our own resolutions. The United States took a very measured step last night. We are prepared to do more, but we hope that will not be necessary. It is time for all civilized nations to stop the horrors that are taking place in Syria and demand a political solution.[19]

Presidential Authority to Strike Syria Under U.S. Law[20]

In an April 8, 2017, letter to Congress, President Trump stated that he had acted "pursuant to my constitutional authority to conduct foreign relations and as Commander in Chief and Chief Executive" in ordering the April 6, 2017, U.S. missile strikes on Al Shayrat airbase in Syria. In the letter, President Trump says that he "acted in the vital national security and foreign policy interests of the United States," and that, "the United States will take additional action, as necessary and appropriate, to further its important national interests." On April 6, the President said he ordered the strikes to protect the "vital national security interest of the United States to prevent and deter the spread and use of deadly chemical weapons." The April 8 letter expands upon this explanation.[21] In the past, Presidents have justified the use of military force by relying on presidential powers they assert are inherent under Article II Commander in Chief and Chief Executive authority, claiming that a President may use military force to defend U.S. national security interests (even when an immediate threat to the United States and its Armed Forces is not necessarily apparent) and to promote U.S. foreign policy.

In 2013, the Senate Foreign Relations Committee considered and reported a proposed authorization for the use of military force following a chemical weapons attack in the suburbs of Damascus, Syria (S.J.Res. 21). The Senate did not consider the measure further.

Since U.S. military action against the Islamic State began in June 2014, starting in Iraq and then spreading to Syria, Congress has debated the need for enactment of a new IS-specific authorization for use of military force. President Obama eventually asserted that the campaign against the Islamic State in Iraq and Syria was authorized by both the Authorization for Use of Military Force (2001 AUMF; P.L. 107-40; claiming that the Islamic State was a successor

---

[18] Megan Scully and Rachel Oswald, "No Plans for Future Strikes, White House Tells Lawmakers," *CQ Roll Call*, April 7, 2017.

[19] U.S. Permanent Representative to the United Nations Ambassador Nikki Haley, Remarks at a U.N. Security Council Meeting on the Situation in Syria, April 7, 2017.

[20] Prepared by Matthew Weed, Specialist in Foreign Policy Legislation.

[21] The letter says the strikes were intended "to degrade the Syrian military's ability to conduct further chemical weapons attacks and to dissuade the Syrian regime from using or proliferating chemical weapons, thereby promoting the stability of the region and averting a worsening of the region's current humanitarian catastrophe."

organization of Al Qaeda and that elements of Al Qaeda were present in Syria) and Authorization for Use of Military Force Against Iraq Resolution of 2002 (2002 AUMF; P.L. 107-243; claiming authority to defend Iraq from the Islamic State threat). Neither the 2001 or 2002 AUMFs, nor any IS-specific AUMF proposals, however, have been interpreted to authorize the use of military force against the Asad regime in Syria.

Figure 1. Syria: Areas of Influence

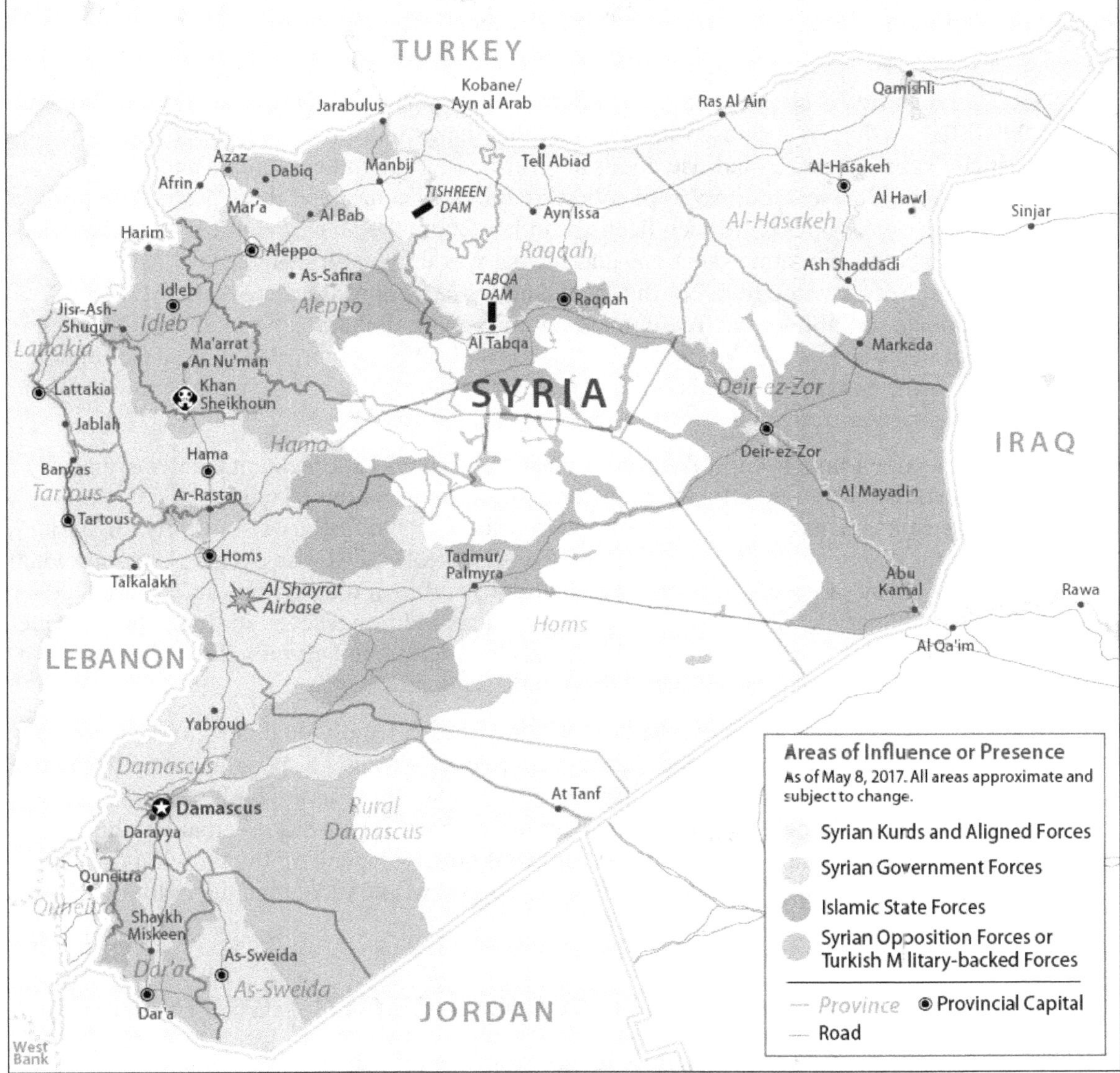

Source: CRS using area of influence data from IHS Conflict Monitor, last revised May 8, 2017. *All areas of influence approximate and subject to change.* Other sources include U.N. OCHA, Esri, and social media reports.

Sanctions on the Syrian Scientific Studies and Research Center[22]

On April 24, the U.S. Department of the Treasury designated 271 employees of the Syrian Scientific Studies and Research Center (SSRC) as Specially Designated Nationals (SDNs) in response to the April 4 attack on Khan Sheikhoun.[23] The SSRC is responsible for developing and producing Syria's nonconventional weapons and the means to deliver them. It is not known what, if any, direct role the newly designated individuals may have played in the April 4 attack. The designation states that "these 271 SSRC employees have expertise in chemistry and related disciplines and/or have worked in support of SSRC's chemical weapons program since at least 2012."

The SSRC, as an entity, is already heavily restricted. In early 2005, the Department of Commerce placed the SSRC on the Syria Entity List, meaning that the export of any controlled goods or services (including munitions, dual-use goods and services, high-end computers and other technology that could have a military application) requires a license, and there is a presumption of denial that Commerce would issue such licenses. In late 2006, the Department of State identified the SSRC as subject to economic sanctions under what was then the Iran and Syria Nonproliferation Act (now the Iran, North Korea, and Syria Nonproliferation Act, or INKSNA). Sanctions include a prohibition on procurement contracts with the U.S. government, no foreign aid, no sales or licenses for U.S. Munitions List goods and services (correlating with Commerce's earlier ruling). State has reiterated this ruling a number of times, and has designated subsidiaries of the SSRC for similar restrictions.

In July 2016, the Department of the Treasury's Financial Crimes Enforcement Center (FinCEN) designated FBME Bank Ltd. as a financial institution of primary money laundering concern, largely because of its clients serving as front organizations for the SSRC. Also in July 2016, the Department of the Treasury's Office of Foreign Assets Control (OFAC) designated one individual and a number of subsidiaries of the SSRC for sanctions that block transactions and freeze U.S.-based assets. On January 12, 2017, Treasury designated an additional seven individuals associated with the SSRC to prohibit transactions and block assets. And in late February 2017, Treasury added an additional entity associated with SSRC to the sanctions list.

It is not known through open sources whether the additional 271 individual designees associated with the SSRC have assets in the United States or transactions with U.S. persons (activities that are the targets of the new sanctions). It is also unclear whether these individuals were previously subject to SSRC sanctions because of their association with the organization—making this new designation largely redundant. This determination would likely depend on the individuals' financial relationship with the SSRC and on whether OFAC would recognize the individuals as financial beneficiaries or owners of the SSRC.

Issues for Congress and Select Pending Legislation

Key issues under consideration in Congress relative to Syria include the following:

- What is the United States' overall strategy toward the Syria conflict in general and toward the Asad government and Islamic State in Syria in particular?

---

[22] Prepared with the assistance of Dianne Rennack, Specialist in Foreign Policy Legislation.

[23] "Treasury Sanctions 271 Syrian Scientific Studies and Research Center Staff in Response to Sarin Attack on Khan Sheikhoun," Press Release, U.S. Department of the Treasury, April 24, 2017.

- What domestic and international authority exists for the use of U.S. military force in Syria against various adversaries?

- What authorities and funding should be provided for U.S. assistance to Syrians, including assistance to opposition elements?

- What might be the second- and third-order effects of the U.S decision to strike Syrian military targets in retaliation for the use of chemical weapons? What implications might that strike have for other U.S. military operations in Syria or for diplomatic efforts to bring an end to the conflict? How, if at all, should the United States respond to any future chemical weapons attacks in Syria?

- How, if at all, should the United States respond to calls for a no-fly zone or safe zones for the protection of civilians in areas of Syria?

- How can the United States exert additional pressure on the Syrian government to reduce the level of violence?

- To what extent should the United States seek cooperation with Russia and Iran in order to promote a political settlement and reduce levels of violence? With Turkey, Jordan, and the Arab Gulf States? How might greater U.S. confrontation with Russia and/or Iran shape developments in Syria?

These issues are discussed in more detail below (see "U.S. Policy and Assistance").

Select Proposed Syria-Related Legislation

S.Res. 116, Condemning the Assad regime for its continued use of chemical weapons against the Syrian people. Following the April 4, 2017, chemical weapons attack in Syria, several members of the Senate Foreign Relations Committee submitted a proposed resolution that, inter alia, would condemn Asad and Russia and call on the United Nations Security Council to take immediate, decisive action in response. The proposed resolution "reiterates that Bashar al-Assad has lost legitimacy as Syria's leader" and "insists that Bashar al-Assad must be held accountable for his war crimes and crimes against humanity."

H.R. 1923. Introduced April 5, 2017; would state that the President is prohibited from using members of the Armed Forces "to carry out offensive combat operations in Syria unless Congress has enacted a specific authorization for such use of members of the Armed Forces."

Caesar Syria Civilian Protection Act. H.R. 1677, introduced by Representatives Royce and Engel (and others) on April 6, 2017, was referred to the Committees on Foreign Affairs, Financial Services, and the Judiciary. The bill updates and amends legislation (H.R. 5732) adopted by the House in the 114th Congress, incorporating provisions from other proposed legislation and appearing to address some concerns expressed by various Syria policy stakeholders. On May 3, the House Foreign Affairs Committee marked up the bill and considered an Amendment in the Nature of a Substitute (ANS) offered by Representative Engel, reporting it to the House on May 11.

As amended, H.R. 1677 would state that "It is the policy of the United States that all diplomatic and coercive economic means should be utilized to compel the government of Bashar al-Assad to immediately halt the wholesale slaughter of the Syrian people and to support an immediate transition to a democratic government in Syria that respects the rule of law, human rights, and peaceful co-existence with its neighbors." The bill would authorize the imposition of certain sanctions by the President and amend current law to require the President to impose other sanctions on individuals he designates as eligible. The bill would require the President to submit an updated report on individuals alleged to be responsible for "serious human rights abuses" in

Syria, which the bill would amend current law to define. In defining "serious human rights abuses" and requiring the Administration to report on the responsibility of dozens of named individuals for such abuses, the bill appears to create a dynamic that would make it more difficult for the executive branch to decline to designate Syrian individuals for human rights-based sanctions.

The bill would expand the potential scope of existing U.S. sanctions on Syria by making eligible for sanctions parties engaged in certain transactions with or the provision of support to the Government of Syria. Current executive orders impose such sanctions, in some cases. The sanctions authorized in the bill could be imposed on individuals determined by the President to have met designated criteria because of knowing engagement in actions "on or after" the date of enactment. The sanctions would thus be prospective rather than retrospective. The sanctions authorized could be imposed on U.S. nationals and non-nationals. A large number of individuals are already subject to U.S. Syria-related sanctions and in some cases individuals may already be subject to U.S. sanctions for engaging in transactions with sanctioned individuals, including entities in Russia and Iran that provide military support to the Syrian government.

The bill would require within 90 days a report that assesses the potential effectiveness, risks, and operational requirements of the establishment and maintenance of a no-fly zone over part or all of Syria and the establishment of one or more safe zones in Syria for internally displaced persons or for the facilitation of humanitarian assistance. It would also codify authorization for certain services in support of nongovernmental organizations activities in Syria.

The bill includes a national security waiver and negotiation or transition scenario-specific waiver authorities for the President. Its provisions would expire after December 31, 2021.

Preventing Destabilization of Iraq and Syria Act. In December 2016, Senators Marco Rubio and Robert Casey introduced S. 3536, known as the Preventing Destabilization of Iraq and Syria Act of 2016. The bill incorporated many aspects of H.R. 5732, including the requirement for the imposition of sanctions on the Central Bank of Syria as well as on foreign individuals that provide support for the Syrian government or for the maintenance or expansion of natural gas and petroleum production in Syria. In addition, it would have required the imposition of sanctions on Syrians complicit in the blocking of humanitarian aid. The bill also would have authorized the President to provide enhanced support for humanitarian activities in Syria, including the provision of food, shelter, water, health care, and medical supplies. It would have prohibited the President from imposing sanctions on a foreign financial institution for engaging in a transaction with the Central Bank of Syria for the sale of food, medicine, medical devices, donations intended to relieve human suffering, or nonlethal aid to the people of Syria. It further would have prohibited the President from imposing sanctions on internationally recognized humanitarian organizations for engaging in financial transactions related to the provision of humanitarian assistance, or for having incidental contact (in the course of providing humanitarian aid) with individuals under the control of foreign persons subject to sanctions under the act.

In January 2017, Senators Rubio and Casey reissued the bill as S. 138, known as the Preventing Destabilization of Iraq and Syria Act of 2017.

Stop Arming Terrorists Act. In January 2017, Representative Tulsi Gabbard introduced H.R. 608, known as the Stop Arming Terrorists Act. The bill would prohibit funds made available to any federal department or agency from being used to provide covered assistance to Al Qaeda and the Islamic State, or to any individual or group that is affiliated with, associated with, or cooperating with adherents of these groups. It would also prohibit direct or indirect covered assistance to countries that have provided assistance to Al Qaeda or the Islamic State, or to any individuals or groups affiliated with, associated with, or cooperating with adherents of these groups. Covered assistance is defined as defense articles, services, training, logistical support, or any other military assistance. It also includes intelligence sharing and cash assistance. The Director of National Intelligence (DNI) would make the initial determination of which groups have an affiliation or association with Al Qaeda and the Islamic State, and which countries provide assistance to those groups. In March 2017, Senator Rand Paul introduced the bill in the Senate as S. 532.

Conflict Synopsis

2011: Protests Emerge. In March 2011, protests broke out in the southern province of Dar'a. The unrest was sparked by the arrest of a group of school children, but reflected long-standing political and socioeconomic grievances. Largely peaceful protesters called for political and economic reforms rather than the removal of the Asad government. At the same time, a small armed element was also present within some of the protests. As security forces responded with mass arrests and occasionally opened fire on demonstrators, protests became larger and spread to other towns and provinces.

The opposition movement eventually coalesced into two umbrella groups—one political, one armed—and both based primarily in exile. Political groups merged to form the Syrian National Council (SNC), although members struggled to establish trust and develop shared goals. A small number of junior military defectors formed the Free Syrian Army (FSA), which claimed leadership over the armed opposition but whose authority was generally unrecognized by local armed groups. Ongoing violence, primarily but not exclusively on the part of the Syrian government, prompted President Obama in August 2011 to call for Syrian President Asad to step aside. Meanwhile Al Qaeda's affiliate in Iraq tasked some of its members to commence operations in Syria under the banner of a new group known as Jabhat al Nusra (aka the Nusra Front). In December 2011, the first Nusra Front suicide attacks hit government buildings in downtown Damascus.

2012: Insurgency. In 2012, the conflict became increasingly violent, as the government began to use artillery and fixed wing aircraft against opposition targets. Extremist attacks became more frequent—between November 2011 and December 2012, the Nusra Front claimed responsibility for nearly 600 attacks in Syria, ranging from more than 40 suicide attacks to small arms and improvised explosive device operations.[24] In February 2012, the United States closed its embassy in Damascus, citing security concerns. Local armed groups began to seize pockets of territory around the country, primarily in rural areas. A July bombing in downtown Damascus killed several senior regime officials, including the then-Minister of Defense. Concerns about regime tactics became more acute, and President Obama in August declared that

> We have been very clear to the Assad regime, but also to other players on the ground, that a red line for us is we start seeing a whole bunch of chemical weapons moving around or being utilized.... We have communicated in no uncertain terms with every player in the region that that's a red line for us and that there would be enormous consequences if we start seeing movement on the chemical weapons front or the use of chemical weapons.[25]

---

[24] "Terrorist Designations of the al-Nusrah Front as an Alias for al-Qa'ida in Iraq," Press Statement by State Department Spokesperson Victoria Nuland, December 11, 2012.

[25] President Barack Obama, Remarks by the President to the White House Press Corps, August 20, 2012.

The international community also increased efforts to seek a negotiated solution to the conflict. In June, the United States and Russia signed the Geneva Communiqué, which called for the establishment of a transitional governing body with full executive powers.[26] The document, which became the basis of future negotiations between the government and the opposition, did not clarify the role of Asad in any future government. Meanwhile, Syria's political opposition remained divided and in flux. In November, the SNC became part of a larger umbrella group known as the National Coalition of Syrian Revolutionary and Opposition Forces (aka the Syrian Opposition Coalition, SOC), a move which some described as an effort to dilute the influence of Islamist members.

2013: Proxy War and Chemical Weapons. In March 2013, rebels seized the city of Raqqah, which became the first provincial capital to fall out of government control. A series of other opposition victories in the area led the government to effectively concede control of Syria's rural northeast to the opposition. At the same time, the Asad government received military and intelligence support from Iran and Lebanese Hezbollah, as well as political backing from Russia. In turn, the United States, Turkey, and some European and Arab Gulf states increased their support to the Syrian opposition—each prioritizing their own interests and at times working at cross purposes.

In April, the United Kingdom and France reported to the United Nations that there was evidence that the Syrian government had used chemical weapons (CW) on multiple occasions since December 2012.[27] In August, the United States attributed a large-scale CW attack on the Damascus suburb of Ghouta to the Syrian government.[28] President Obama requested congressional approval of a limited authorization for the use of military force to respond.[29] The following month, Russia negotiated an agreement for the Syrian government to dispose of its CW stockpiles and destroy associated facilities in exchange for staving off a U.S. military response.

2014: Caliphate and Operation Inherent Resolve. In February 2014, Al Qaeda formally disavowed the Islamic State because of the group's interference in Syria and its demands that the Nusra Front recognize IS leadership. After the Nusra Front and other opposition groups forced IS fighters from some areas of northwestern Syria, IS fighters seized vast stretches of territory in central and northeast Syria from local armed groups and in June declared the establishment of a caliphate spanning areas of both Syria and Iraq. Thousands of foreign fighters traveled to Syria and Iraq to join the Islamic State.

In August, the United States began air strikes in neighboring Iraq to stop the group's territorial advance and reduce the threat to U.S. personnel in Iraq. U.S. forces also airdropped humanitarian supplies to members of Iraq's Yazidi religious minority group trapped on Mount Sinjar. In September, the United States expanded air strikes to Syria, with the goal of preventing the Islamic

---

[26] Action Group for Syria, Final Communiqué, June 30, 2012.

[27] Letter dated 22 March 2013 from the Secretary-General addressed to the President of the Security Council, U.N. Document S/2013/184, March 22, 2013.

[28] The White House, Government Assessment of the Syrian Government's Use of Chemical Weapons on August 21, 2013, August 30, 2013. United Nations investigations confirmed that a chemical attack took place but its September and December 2013 reports did not address attribution. See U.N. Document A/67/997–S/2013/553, Report of the United Nations Mission to Investigate Allegations of the Use of Chemical Weapons in the Syrian Arab Republic on the alleged use of chemical weapons in the Ghouta area of Damascus on 21 August 2013, September 16, 2013; and, United Nations Mission to Investigate Allegations of the Use of Chemical Weapons in the Syrian Arab Republic, Final Report, December 2013.

[29] President Barack Obama, Remarks by the President Before Meeting with Members of Congress on the Situation in Syria, September 3, 2013.

State from using Syria as a base for its operations in Iraq. A subsequent air campaign to lift the IS siege on the Syrian Kurdish town of Kobane brought the United States into partnership with the Kurdish People's Protection Units (YPG), which U.S. officials have come to view as among the United States' most effective partners in the anti-IS campaign. In September 2014, Congress authorized the Administration to begin a train and equip program for select Syrian forces.[30]

2015: Train & Equip Begins, Russia Enters the Fray. In 2015, the Syrian government faced a number of additional territorial losses. Opposition forces captured the provincial capital of Idlib in northwestern Syria and surrounding areas with the support of Al Qaeda-linked fighters. Islamic State fighters seized territory in central Homs province, and Kurdish fighters expanded their control over areas along the Turkish border. In May, the United States began training the first batch of recruits for the Syria Train and Equip Program. The program was designed to build a local force capable of fighting the Islamic State, protecting opposition-held areas, and "promoting the conditions for a negotiated settlement to end the conflict in Syria."

Over the summer of 2015, Russia began a gradual buildup of Russian personnel, combat aircraft, and military equipment inside Syria, and began air strikes in September. The following month, the United States and Russia signed a memorandum of understanding to establish a safety-of-flight protocol for aircraft operating in the same airspace. Also in October, challenges in implementation led the Administration to modify the Syria Train and Equip program to focus on equipping existing units commanded by vetted leaders. Kurdish YPG forces that had received U.S. support in operations at Kobane merged with a small number of non-Kurdish groups to form the Syrian Democratic Forces (SDF), which began to receive U.S. support.

2016: Failed cessation of hostilities, regime retakes Aleppo. In 2016, the United States sought to step up diplomatic cooperation with Russia to achieve a reduction in violence. The two countries twice attempted to implement a joint diplomatic initiative for a cessation of hostilities (CoH) between pro-government and opposition forces, yet both initiatives were widely considered unsuccessful. In contrast, the U.S.-led campaign against the Islamic State retook significant territory from the group, severing much of the group's access to the Turkish border—a key supply and foreign fighter transit route. However, the heavy participation of Syrian Kurdish fighters in counter-IS operations triggered Turkish opposition, and in August Turkish forces crossed the Syrian border into the town of Jarabulus, in an operation described by Turkish officials as aimed at neutralizing threats posed by both the Islamic State and Kurdish fighters. Meanwhile, Syrian and Russian forces—backed by Hezbollah, foreign Shia militias, and Iranian forces—increased the intensity of attacks on rebel-held eastern Aleppo, resulting in thousands of deaths. In December 2016, the Syrian government recaptured eastern Aleppo from opposition forces, and Russia and Turkey reached agreement on a proposed cease-fire to be followed by negotiations (see "The Astana Process" below).

Russia's Military Intervention

Russian military involvement in Syria dates back to the 1950s. Soviet and Russian Federation naval forces have accessed a facility at the Syrian port of Tartus since the early 1970s, using it as a logistical hub to enable longer Mediterranean operations. Syria eventually became the largest

---

[30] The FY2015 Continuing Resolution (P.L. 113-164, "the FY2015 CR") contained temporary authorization for the training and equipping of vetted Syrians that differed from the Administration's requests and expired on December 11, 2014. The FY2015 NDAA (Sections 1209, 1510, and 1534 of Division A of P.L. 113-291) and the Consolidated and Further Continuing Appropriations Act, 2015 ('Counterterrorism Partnership Fund' and Section 9016 of P.L. 113-235) provided further authority and funding guidance for the program.

Middle East recipient of Russian equipment and training. While Russian personnel have since been based in Syria to maintain Russia military equipment and train Syrians, their numbers have fluctuated over time.

With the onset of unrest in 2011, Russia provided sustained political, economic, and military support to the Syrian government. Russian diplomats blocked action in the U.N. Security Council that would have increased pressure on the Asad regime for its conduct. In 2012, Russia began printing Syrian banknotes after European sanctions prevented Syria's currency from being printed in Austria. After the chemical attacks outside Damascus in 2013, Russia negotiated an agreement whereby the Syrian government relinquished its chemical weapons, avoiding proposed U.S. military strikes. Throughout the conflict, Russia has continued to resupply Syrian military forces, although Russian officials have stated that they are merely fulfilling existing bilateral contracts.

Over the summer of 2015, Russia began a gradual buildup of personnel, combat aircraft, and military equipment inside Syria. In September of that year, Russian forces began air strikes inside Syria, initially focused on opposition targets—including some groups reportedly backed by the United States.[31] In 2016, Russia expanded its targeting to include Islamic State forces, although it continued to occasionally target U.S.-backed rebel groups.[32]

The series of losses suffered by Syrian government forces in 2015 may have contributed to Russia's decision to enter the conflict directly when it did. Russian concerns about U.S. and other third-party security assistance to Syrian opposition groups, and the potential for broader U.S.-led coalition military operations in Syria, also may have been motivating factors. Russia remains an outspoken critic of what it describes as unwarranted external interference aimed at regime change in Syria and elsewhere.

Russian ground forces in Syria have not played a significant combat role and appear to be focused primarily on defending Russian bases and installations in Syria—although some are likely embedded as advisors with Syrian military forces. To date, air strikes have constituted Russia's primary military effort in Syria. These strikes have enabled pro-Asad forces to reverse some opposition gains, particularly around Aleppo. Russia's introduction of advanced air defense systems in Syria (reportedly including the S-300 and S-400) constrains the ability of other aircraft to operate freely in the area—complicating proposals calling for the establishment of a no-fly zone. At the same time, Russia has pushed for cooperation between U.S. and Russian military forces in Syria against terrorist groups—which in Russia's view includes any group fighting the Asad government. Reports have periodically suggested that Russia plans to withdraw some military forces from Syria, but available evidence suggests Russian military personnel remain present and active in the country.

Recent Developments

Military

SDF Operations to Isolate Raqqah

On November 6, 2016, the SDF began the first stage of a campaign (dubbed "Euphrates Wrath") to isolate Raqqah city, the self-declared capital of the Islamic State. Lieutenant General Stephen

---

[31] "Russians Strike Targets in Syria, but Not ISIS Areas," *New York Times*, September 30, 2015.

[32] "Russia's attack on U.S.-backed rebels in Syria puzzles, frustrates the Pentagon," *Military Times*, June 23, 2016.

Townsend, Commander of Operation Inherent Resolve (OIR), said that the operation was urgent largely because of the coalition's interest in preventing IS fighters (including those fleeing Mosul) from regrouping in Raqqah and carrying out potential external attacks.[33] As of early May, U.S. military officials estimated that 3,000 to 4,000 IS fighters remained inside Raqqah.[34]

Participants. The SDF has led the operation to isolate Raqqah city. Established in late 2015 as an umbrella group largely led by and made up of Kurdish YPG fighters, the SDF has adjusted its forces over time to more closely reflect the demographics in its areas of operation. In May, an OIR spokesperson stated that the SDF numbered approximately 50,000 fighters, divided almost evenly between Syrian Kurds and Syrian Arabs.[35]

Turkey considers the YPG and its political parent organization (the Democratic Union Party, or PYD) to be the Syrian arm of the Kurdistan Workers Party (PKK), which both Turkey and the United States have designated as a terrorist group. Turkey appears to view the YPG as the top threat to its security, given the operational and moral support YPG military and political success could provide to the PKK's insurgency within Turkey.[36] The United States does not view the PYD/YPG as a terrorist organization.[37] However, a number of sources point to evidence of close and continuing operational and personnel links between the PKK and PYD/YPG.[38]

The Syrian Arab Coalition (SAC) is a term used by U.S. military officials to describe ethnic Arab elements of the SDF. There are few publicly available details on which individual groups constitute the SAC.[39] U.S. officials and other observers acknowledge that the YPG continues to play a leading role in SDF operations.[40]

U.S. Role. The United States provides wide-ranging support to SDF operations against the Islamic State in Raqqah. In early March, General Townsend estimated that the United States had provided training for roughly 4,000 Arab forces within the SDF.[41]The United States has also provided air support to the SDF since the onset of Euphrates Wrath,[42] as well as small arms, ammunition, supplies, and equipment. Prior to May 2017, U.S. officials stated that weapons had

---

[33] Department of Defense Press Briefing by Lt. Gen. Townsend Via Teleconference from Baghdad, Iraq, October 26, 2016.

[34] Department of Defense Press Briefing by Col. Dorrian via teleconference from Baghdad, Iraq, May 3, 2017.

[35] Ibid.

[36] Aaron Stein and Michelle Foley, "The YPG-PKK Connection," Atlantic Council, January 26, 2016; Amberin Zaman, "Ankara Intensifies Strikes Against YPG, Moves to Arrest PYD Leader," *Al Monitor Turkey Pulse*, November 22, 2016.

[37] In an April, 28, 2016, Senate hearing, Secretary of Defense Ash Carter appeared to answer "yes" to a question on whether the YPG has ties to the PKK, but he later reiterated that the YPG is not a designated terrorist organization.

[38] Stein and Foley, op. cit. One such source claims that although the PYD and PKK are officially independent, "in practice, Syrian Kurdish PKK cadres with years of service in Qandil (the organisation's northern Iraqi mountain base) dominate the YPG leadership and are the decision-makers within the self-proclaimed 'autonomous administration'" in Syria.

[39] See, for example, "Syrian Opposition Figure to Deploy All-Arab Force in Raqqa Offensive," *Reuters*, February 1, 2017.

[40] Department of Defense Briefing by Gen. Townsend via Telephone from Baghdad, Iraq, March 28, 2017; Amberin Zaman, "Tillerson Leaves Ankara with No New Enemies—or Friends," *Al-Monitor Turkey Pulse*, March 30, 2017; Suleiman Al-Khalidi, "U.S.-Backed Forces Repel Islamic State Attack near Syrian Dam," *Reuters*, April 2, 2017. For more information, see CRS Report R43612, *The Islamic State and U.S. Policy*, by Christopher M. Blanchard and Carla E. Humud.

[41] Department of Defense Press Briefing by Gen. Townsend via teleconference from Baghdad, Iraq, March 1, 2017.

[42] Department of Defense Press Briefing by Pentagon Press Secretary Peter Cook in the Pentagon Briefing Room, November 10, 2016.

been provided only to the non-Kurdish elements within the SDF,[43] although one media report cited a U.S. defense official saying that the YPG had already acquired sophisticated U.S.-origin night-operating gear via "other means by other sources."[44]

Some U.S. troops have been colocated with SDF forces in Raqqah since late 2015. A small contingent of 50 U.S. Special Forces initially deployed to northern Syria in October 2015 to support operations against the Islamic State. In April 2016, their numbers were increased by 250. On December 10, then-Defense Secretary Carter announced that the force management level (FML) for U.S. personnel in Syria would be increased to potentially allow the deployment of up to 500 individuals, including special operations forces trainers, advisors, and explosive ordnance disposal teams.[45] U.S. officials have

In March 2017, roughly 300 members of the 11th Marine Expeditionary Unit deployed to Syria to assist SDF operations in Raqqah; an additional 100 Army Ranger forces deployed to the city of Manbij in Aleppo province.[46] Although the FML caps the number of U.S. forces in Syria at 503, a U.S. military spokesperson stated that the deployment of the Marines to Raqqah was an example of the ability of coalition leaders to "bring in capabilities on a temporary basis to meet specific objectives."[47] The Marines have provided heavy artillery support to SDF operations, such as the successful operation in late March to seize Tabqa airfield.[48]

Arming Syrian Kurds

On May 9, the Pentagon released a statement saying that President Trump has authorized it "to equip Kurdish elements of the [SDF] as necessary to ensure a clear victory over ISIS in Raqqa."[49] Partly in response to Turkish sensitivities about the possibility for YPG elements to aid PKK operations against government personnel in Turkey, the Pentagon spokesperson for anti-IS operations (aka Operation Inherent Resolve) indicated in a briefing that U.S. arms transfers to Kurdish forces would be "metered out" for specific operations, with the flow monitored to prevent the arms' diversion.[50] While President Erdogan and other Turkish officials responded to the May 9 statement with strong criticism, Secretary of Defense Jim Mattis said on May 10 that U.S. officials would work to address Turkish concerns regarding security at its southern border.[51] Media reports indicate that an effort is underway to bolster U.S.-Turkey cooperation in countering PKK militants in Turkey and Iraq,[52] and observers speculate on the possibility

---

[43] Department of Defense Press Briefing by Col. Dorrian via teleconference from Baghdad, Iraq, February 22, 2017.

[44] Shawn Snow, "Syrian Kurds are now armed with sensitive US weaponry, and the Pentagon denies supplying it," *Military Times*, May 7, 2017.

[45] Remarks by Secretary Carter at the 2016 IISS Manama Dialogue, Manama, Bahrain, December 10, 2016.

[46] "U.S. Is Sending 400 More Troops to Syria," *New York Times*, March 9, 2017.

[47] Department of Defense Press Briefing by Col. Dorrian via teleconference from Baghdad, Iraq, March 15, 2017.

[48] Department of Defense Briefing by Gen. Townsend via Telephone from Baghdad, Iraq, March 28, 2017.

[49] Pentagon statement quoted in Michael R. Gordon, "Trump to Arm Syrian Kurds, Even as Turkey Strongly Objects," *New York Times*, May 9, 2017. See also CRS Report R44513, *Kurds in Iraq and Syria: U.S. Partners Against the Islamic State*, coordinated by Jim Zanotti. For information on U.S. authorities to train and equip select armed Syrian groups to fight the Islamic State, see CRS Report R43612, *The Islamic State and U.S. Policy*, by Christopher M. Blanchard and Carla E. Humud. One media report said that the Pentagon plan would provide YPG forces with "small arms, ammunition and machine guns." Gordon Lubold et al., "U.S., Turkey Boost Antiterror Cooperation," *Wall Street Journal*, May 11, 2017. Another said that weapons provided would include "heavy machine guns, mortars, anti-tank weapons, armored cars and engineering equipment." Michael R. Gordon and Eric Schmitt, "Trump to Arm Syrian Kurds, Even as Turkey Strongly Objects," *New York Times*, May 9, 2017.

[50] "Turkey Assails U.S. Decision to Arm Syrian Kurds," *New York Times*, May 11, 2017.

[51] "Turkey furious at US decision to arm Syrian Kurdish group," *Hurriyet Daily News*, May 10, 2017; "Anti-terror fight should not be carried out with other terror groups: Erdoğan," *Hurriyet Daily News*, May 10, 2017.

[52] Lubold et al., op. cit.

---

of future Turkish military action (perhaps coordinated with Iraqi Kurdish peshmerga) against a PKK outpost in the Iraqi region of Sinjar.[53]

Figure 2. Raqqah Operations

As of May 16, 2017

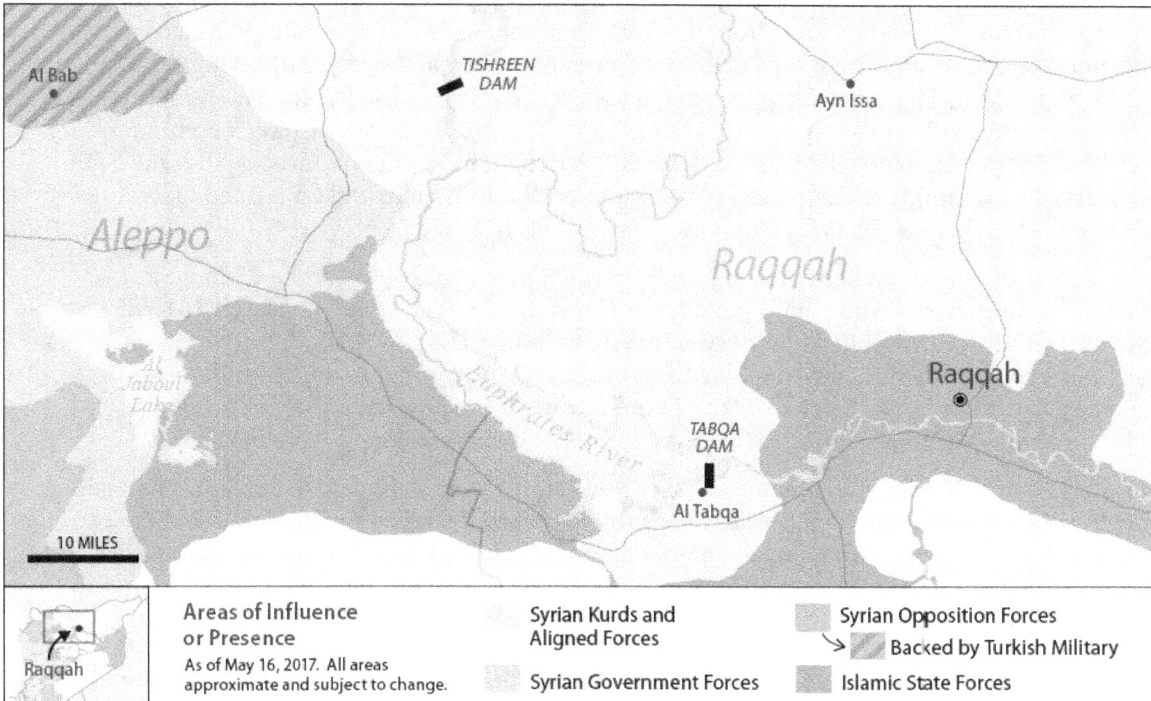

Source: Areas of influence based on May 16, 2017, data from IHS Conflict Monitor, and adapted by CRS based on media accounts.

Progress to Date. On December 10, 2016, the SDF announced the second phase of Euphrates Wrath. In late 2016, some IS fighters reportedly relocated to the Syrian province of Dayr az Zawr near the Iraqi border, in response to coalition pressure around Mosul and Raqqah.[54] On February 4, 2017, the SDF announced the third phase of the operation, which has reportedly focused on severing the main ground line of communication between the cities of Raqqah and Dayr az Zawr. In late March, U.S. military leaders reported that the SDF had completely isolated the area to the east of Raqqah and were working to seize both the Tabqa Dam and the city of Al Tabqa, located to the west of Raqqah.[55] According to a U.S. military spokesperson, "seizing Tabqa dam will isolate Raqqa from three sides and give the SDF a strategic advantage and the launching point they need to liberate the city."[56] In May, SDF forces captured Tabqa Dam, as well as Al Tabqa

---

[53] Anne Barnard and Patrick Kingsley, "Arming Syrian Kurds Could Come at a Cost," *New York Times*, May 11, 2017. The PKK has built up the outpost since helping to oust the Islamic State from the area in late 2015.

[54] Maria Abi-Habib and Nour Alakraa, "Islamic State Fortifies Post," *Wall Street Journal*, December 3, 2016.

[55] Department of Defense Briefing by Gen. Townsend via Telephone from Baghdad, Iraq, March 28, 2017.

[56] "Local Forces Launch Daring Assault Behind Enemy Lines in Syria," *DoD News*, March 22, 2017, http://www.centcom.mil.

city.[57] The Pentagon the same month stated that "the SDF, partnered with enabling support from U.S. and coalition forces, are the only force on the ground that can successfully seize Raqqa in the near future."[58]

Ongoing U.S. Presence in Manbij

U.S. military personnel continue to operate in the northern Syrian town of Manbij, located in Aleppo province roughly 40 km from the Turkish border. SDF forces captured Manbij from the Islamic State in August 2016, and coalition forces remained in the city. Following the expulsion of IS forces from Manbij, Turkey expressed concern that Kurdish YPG fighters might retain a permanent presence in the city, putting the group a step closer to establishing a contiguous area of Kurdish control along the Turkish border (see **Figure 3**). Less than two weeks after the SDF operation in Manbij, Turkish forces crossed into northern Syria in what it termed Operation Euphrates Shield (see "Turkish-Supported Operations in Syria," below).

The defeat of Islamic State forces in Manbij created new challenges for the United States, including the issue of who would govern the city. While Russia stated in March 2017 that Syrian government forces would take over government administration in Manbij,[59] governance in the city has been assumed by the Manbij Military Council. According to a U.S. military spokesperson, coalition forces in Manbij continue to "train, advise, assist and accompany" Manbij Military Council forces as they provide security and restore governance.[60]

In early March 2017, approximately 100 Army Rangers were deployed to Manbij. The visible deployment of additional U.S. forces to Manbij appeared designed to deter conflict between rival groups in the vicinity, which include Kurdish, Turkish, Russian, and Syrian forces. In early March, Turkish Foreign Minister Mevlut Cavusoglu stated that Turkey would attack Manbij unless the Kurds withdrew from the city, and Russian-backed Syrian government forces interposed themselves between Turkish-supported forces and Manbij.[61] A U.S. military spokesperson stated that the U.S. presence in Manbij "improves transparency and facilitates communication among all parties in the area to avoid misunderstanding and miscalculation."[62] He acknowledged that U.S. and Russian forces in Manbij are in close enough proximity that they can visually observe one another's movements, and that communication between the two continues to increase via the deconfliction channel.[63]

Turkish-Supported Operations in Syria

Turkish operations inside Syria (known as Operation Euphrates Shield) began in August 2016, and were designed to counter both Islamic State and Kurdish forces operating along Turkey's southern border with Syria.[64] Turkish forces have worked with allied Syrian forces (mostly Arabs

---

[57] Department of Defense Press Briefing by Secretary Mattis, General Dunford and Special Envoy McGurk on the Campaign to Defeat ISIS in the Pentagon Press Briefing Room, May 19, 2017.

[58] "Trump authorizes arms for Syrian Kurds, Pentagon says," *Politico*, May 9, 2017.

[59] "Syrian Regime Forces to Take over Manbij, Says Russia," *Hurriyet Daily News*, March 3, 2017.

[60] Department of Defense Press Briefing by Col. Dorrian via teleconference from Baghdad, Iraq, March 15, 2017.

[61] Amberin Zaman, "Syrian Kurds Cede Buffer as Turkish-Backed FSA Advances on Manbij," *Al-Monitor Turkey Pulse*, March 2, 2017.

[62] Department of Defense Press Briefing by Col. Dorrian via teleconference from Baghdad, Iraq, March 15, 2017.

[63] Department of Defense Press Briefing by Col. Dorrian via teleconference from Baghdad, Iraq, March 15, 2017.

[64] Amberin Zaman, "Turkish Troops Enter Syria to Fight ISIS, May Also Target U.S.-Backed Kurdish Militia," Woodrow Wilson Center, August 24, 2016.

and Turkmen nominally opposed to the Asad regime) to counter IS fighters, but also occasionally clashed with Syrian Kurdish-led forces. In February 2017, Turkish forces partnered with Syrian rebels entered the Syrian town of Al Bab after more than three months of clashes. The town, a key transport hub, had been controlled since 2014 by the Islamic State. In late February, Turkish forces backed by coalition airstrikes recaptured the town.[65] Turkey's incursion into Syria and operations in Al Bab appeared to reflect Turkish concerns that the YPG fighters in Syria could create a contiguous area of Kurdish control along the Turkish border. Manbij and Al Bab are located between two areas (shaded yellow in **Figure 3**) that are largely controlled by Kurdish-led forces and roughly correspond to the "cantons" of Afrin and Kobane subject to Syrian Kurdish political claims.

Figure 3. Syria-Turkey Border

As of May 8, 2017

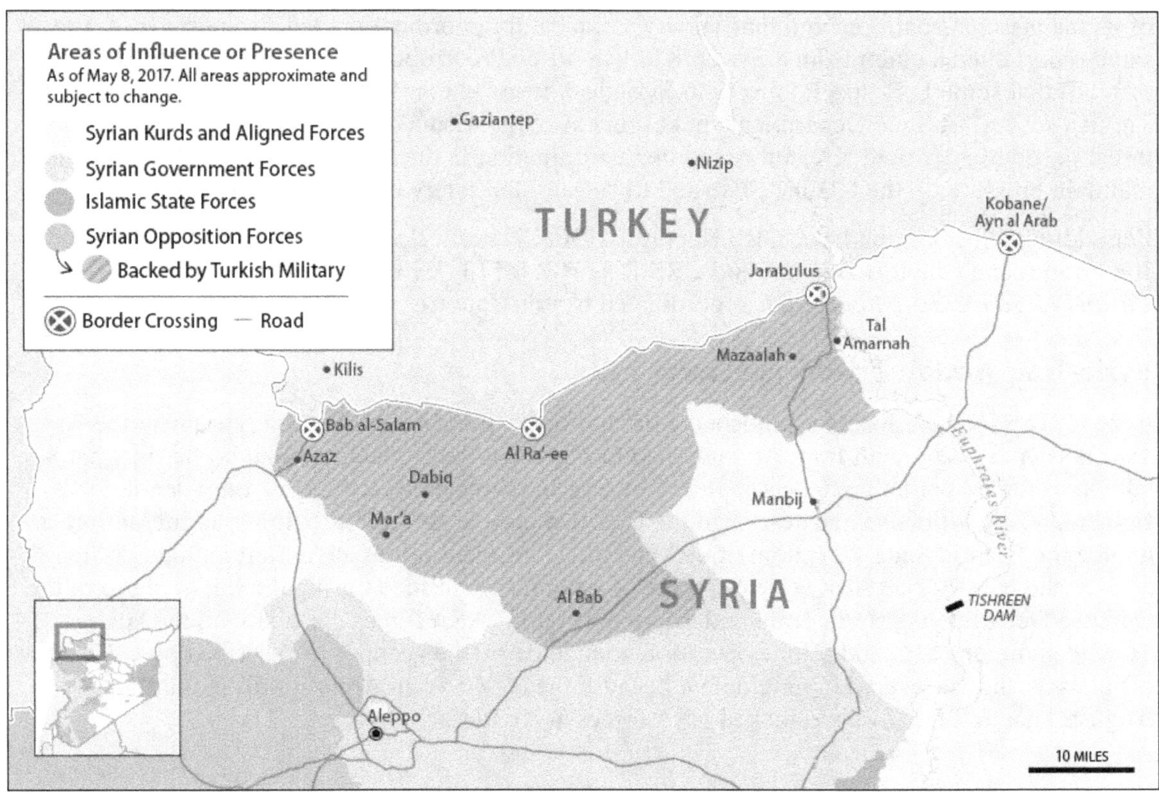

Source: Areas of influence based on data from IHS Conflict Monitor, and adapted by CRS based on media accounts. Other sources include U.N. OCHA and Esri.

In late March 2017, Turkish leaders announced that Operation Euphrates Shield had been "successfully completed," but did not specify when or if Turkish troops would withdraw from Syria.[66] Turkish Prime Minister Yildirim noted that Turkey could launch further military operations if necessary, under a different name.

---

[65] Department of Defense Press Briefing by Gen. Townsend via teleconference from Baghdad, Iraq, March 1, 2017.

[66] "Turkey Can Start New Operation If Necessary as Euphrates Shield Ends: PM," *Hurriyet Daily News*, March 30, 2017.

On April 25, Turkish aircraft bombed a PYD/YPG outpost in Syria's eastern province of Hasakah as part of a larger operation that also targeted PKK installations in the Sinjar area of northwest Iraq. A YPG spokesperson reported that the Turkish strike killed 20 and wounded 18 others, while Turkey's military stated that the strike's purpose was to prevent the PKK from sending weapons across the border into Turkey.[67] A State Department spokesperson stated

> we are very concerned–deeply concerned–that Turkey conducted airstrikes earlier today in northern Syria, as well as northern Iraq, without proper coordination either with the United States or the broader global coalition to defeat ISIS. And we've expressed those concerns to the Government of Turkey directly. These airstrikes were not approved by the coalition and led to the unfortunate loss of life of our partner forces in the fight against ISIS that includes members of the Kurdish Peshmerga.[68]

The precise timing and details of U.S.-Turkey communications regarding the strike are unclear. One report, citing officials from the U.S.-led coalition, indicated that Turkey gave advance notice of its plans to the coalition, and that Turkey's request for coordination was disapproved.[69] The same report cited a claim from a Syrian Kurdish official (corroborated by an unnamed coalition official) that some U.S. special forces in Syria had been "uncomfortably close" to the site of the Turkish strike.[70] A State Department spokesperson acknowledged Turkey's concerns about the threat posed to it by the PKK, but stated that coordination in the battle space was critical, both to maintain pressure on the Islamic State and to "ensure the safety of all coalition personnel."[71]

For additional background, see CRS Report R41368, *Turkey: Background and U.S. Relations*, by Jim Zanotti and Clayton Thomas, and CRS Report R44513, *Kurds in Iraq and Syria: U.S. Partners Against the Islamic State*, coordinated by Jim Zanotti.

Syria-Iraq-Jordan Tri-border Area

In 2016, U.S.-backed forces established a base of operations in southeastern Syria near the At Tanf border crossing with Iraq. At Tanf, also located near the Syria-Jordanian border in what is known as the tri-border area, was captured by Syrian rebels in March 2016 from Islamic State fighters.[72] OIR officials have described the U.S. presence at At Tanf as helping partnered forces reduce the Islamic State's freedom of movement.[73] Partnered forces at At Tanf include groups such as the New Syrian Army (NSA), some of whom were trained during the initial phase of the Defense Department's Syria Train and Equip program.[74] NSA forces clashed with the Islamic State in summer 2016, and a June operation conducted by the group was described by U.S. officials as "not an overwhelming defeat because the New Syrian Army is still in the fight."[75] In August, Islamic State forces attacked NSA forces at At Tanf.[76]

---

[67] "Turkish jets strike Kurdish fighters in Syria, Iraq's Sinjar," *Reuters*, April 25, 2017.

[68] State Department Press Briefing, April 25, 2017.

[69] "Kurds call on US to set up no-fly zone after Turkish attacks," *Al Monitor*, April 25, 2017.

[70] Ibid.

[71] State Department Press Briefing, April 25, 2017.

[72] "Syrian rebels seize Iraq border crossing from Islamic State: monitor," *Reuters*, March 4, 2016.

[73] Department of Defense Press Briefing by Col. Dorrian via teleconference from Baghdad, Iraq, April 12, 2017.

[74] Department of Defense Press Briefing by Col. Garver via Teleconference From Baghdad, Iraq, July 6, 2016.

[75] Ibid.

[76] "Islamic State hits U.S.-backed Syrian rebel base near Iraq border," Reuters, August 7, 2016.

In April 2017, IS militants again attacked At Tanf, and coalition and partnered Syrian opposition groups repelled the attack.[77] Describing ongoing coalition operations in the area around At Tanf, an OIR spokesperson in early May stated,

> The U.S. and coalition special operations forces continue to advise, assist and accompany vetted Syrian opposition partner forces through the Hamad Desert. Vetted Syrian opposition groups continue to clear ISIS from the towns and villages around the An Tanf border crossing between Iraq and Syria. This secure border facilitates the passage of 500 to 900 people each day, opening up opportunities for local goods to flow in and out of Syria, stimulating the economy for the people.[78]

On May 18, a U.S. airstrike targeted a column of pro-Asad militia fighters advancing toward At Tanf. Defense Secretary Mattis described the U.S. strikes as "self-defense of our forces." Mattis added that the strikes were necessitated by

> offensive movement with offensive capability of what we believe were Iranian-directed—I don't know there were Iranians on the ground, but by Iran-directed force[s] inside an established and agreed-upon deconfliction zone. We believe they moved into that zone against the advice of the Russians.[79]

On May 24, Combined Forces Air Component Commander Lt. Gen. Jeffrey Harrington clarified that the deconfliction zone at At Tanf referenced by U.S. military officials is unrelated to the de-escalation areas of the May 4 Astana agreement between Russia, Iran, and Turkey—to which the United States is not a party. United States has established temporary deconfliction zones in areas where its partner forces are based. Harrington acknowledged the existence of a 55 kilometer deconfliction zone around At Tanf, stating "if the Russians are going to come in there, they're going to call us to give us information about what they would like to do, and we're going to have a discussion about it."

Ongoing operations by Syrian government forces and their Syrian and foreign militia supporters raise the prospect of further confrontation in the area. Syrian officials have announced their intent to push eastward toward Deir-ez Zor to prevent the area from coming under the control of U.S.-backed forces.

Political Negotiations

The Geneva Process

Since 2012, the Syrian government and opposition have participated in U.N.-brokered negotiations under the framework of the Geneva Communiqué. Endorsed by both the United States and Russia, the Geneva Communiqué calls for the establishment of a transitional governing body with full executive powers. According to the document, such a government "could include members of the present government and the opposition and other groups and shall be formed on the basis of mutual consent."[80] The document does not discuss the future of Asad.

---

[77] Department of Defense Press Briefing by Col. Dorrian via teleconference from Baghdad, Iraq, April 12, 2017.

[78] Department of Defense Press Briefing by Col. Dorrian via teleconference from Baghdad, Iraq, May 3, 2017.

[79] Department of Defense Press Briefing by Secretary Mattis, General Dunford and Special Envoy McGurk on the Campaign to Defeat ISIS in the Pentagon Press Briefing Room, May 19, 2017.

[80] Action Group for Syria, Final Communiqué, June 30, 2012, http://www.un.org/News/dh/infocus/Syria/FinalCommuniqueActionGroupforSyria.pdf.

Subsequent negotiations have made little progress, as both sides have adopted differing interpretations of the agreement. The opposition has said that any transitional government must exclude Asad. The Syrian government maintains that Asad was reelected (by referendum) in 2014,[81] and notes that the Geneva Communiqué does not explicitly require him to step down. In the Syrian government's view, a transitional government can be achieved by simply expanding the existing government to include members of the opposition. Asad has also stated that a political transition cannot occur until "terrorism" has been defeated.

In February and March 2017, representatives from the Syrian government and Syrian opposition groups met for two rounds of indirect talks in Geneva, facilitated by U.N. Envoy Staffan de Mistura. The talks did not make significant progress. The last round of talks was held in Geneva on May 16 – 19, and the parties are expected to convene again in June.

The Astana Process

In December 2016, the foreign and defense ministers of Russia, Iran, and Turkey met in Moscow to discuss a political resolution to the Syrian conflict. The parties issued a joint statement, which laid out a set of principles for a future peace deal. While acknowledging that the United States was not asked to participate in the talks, a State Department spokesperson characterized the joint statement as "borrowing […] from ideas that the United States has led and pushed from the outset."[82] On December 29, Russia and Turkey announced a new cease-fire agreement to be followed by peace talks in Kazakhstan within a month, cosponsored by both countries.[83] On December 31, the U.N. Security Council unanimously adopted Resolution 2236, welcoming and supporting the Russian-Turkish initiative. Three rounds of peace talks were subsequently held in the Kazakh capital of Astana, all of which closed with few results. On May 3-4, the fourth round of talks was held at Astana, resulting in the issuance of a memorandum on the creation of de-escalation areas in Syria.

De-escalation Areas. On May 4, representatives of Russia, Iran, and Turkey at Astana signed a memorandum on the creation of "de-escalation areas" inside Syria. The areas are to be located in four non-contiguous parts of Syria: Idlib province and its surroundings, some parts of northern Homs province, eastern Ghouta in the Damascus suburbs, and parts of the southern provinces of Dar'a and Quneitra. The memorandum calls for hostilities between the Syrian government and opposition to cease within the de-escalation areas. The memorandum also calls for unhindered humanitarian access within these areas, as well as measures to restore infrastructure and encourage the voluntary return of refugees and internally displaced persons. Neither the Syrian government nor representatives of Syrian opposition groups signed the memorandum.

Security Zones. The May 4 memorandum also states that, "along the lines of the de-escalation areas, security zones shall be established in order to prevent incidents and military confrontations between the conflicting parties." The security zones are to include checkpoints to ensure "unhindered movement of unarmed civilians" and the delivery of humanitarian aid, as well as observation posts to ensure compliance with the ceasefire. The security zones and the checkpoints and observation posts within them are to be administered by "forces of the Guarantors" (Russia, Turkey, and Iran). The agreement also notes that "third parties" might be deployed for this purpose, with the consensus of the guarantors.

---

[81] "Syrian President Bashar al-Assad Wins Third Term," *BBC*, June 5, 2014.

[82] State Department Daily Press Briefing, December 20, 2016.

[83] Statement on establishing the cease-fire regime in the Syrian Arab Republic, contained in Annex I to U.N. Document S/2016/1133, December 29, 2016.

Next Steps. Within two weeks of signing, the guarantors are to establish a joint working group in order to delineate the lines of the de-escalation areas and security zones, as well as to resolve other operational and technical issues regarding their implementation. By June 4, the group is scheduled to have completed maps of both the de-escalation areas and the security zones. Representatives from Russia, Iran, and Turkey met in Ankara on May 18 for further discussions regarding the de-escalation areas.[84]

Reactions. The agreement, which went into effect on May 5, has reportedly resulted in a reduction—but not cessation—of violence, and clashes have continued in regions expected to form part of the de-escalation areas.[85] The Syrian government has said that it will abide by the agreement if the opposition does, adding that Syria will continue to fight what it describes as terrorist groups. The Syrian High Negotiations Committee, which represents a number of Syrian opposition groups in U.N. brokered talks in Geneva, criticized the agreement as an attempt to "partition the country" and rejected the role of Iran as a guarantor.[86] The State Department issued a statement noting that the United States "supports any effort that can genuinely de-escalate the violence in Syria," but expressing concerns about "the involvement of Iran as a so-called 'guarantor.'"[87]

Remaining Questions.

- **Who will patrol the areas?** The agreement calls for the areas to be administered by forces from the guarantor countries, suggesting that the various de-escalation areas could become de-facto spheres of influence for Russia, Iran, or Turkey—and generate an additional influx of personnel from those countries into Syria. One of Turkey's deputy Prime Ministers has stated that Ankara has been offered the opportunity to administer the de-escalation area in Idlib province, the largest of the proposed areas.[88] The agreement allows for the deployment of third party forces to the security zones by consensus of the guarantors, raising the possibility that militias such as Hezbollah could play a role in some areas.

- **How will the establishment of these areas affect U.S. and coalition operations?** Russian officials have stated that U.S. aircraft are barred from flying over the de-escalation areas—which include parts of Idlib province where CENTCOM has previously conducted strikes against Al Qaeda-affiliated forces, formerly known as the Nusra Front. U.S. officials have said that the agreement will not alter the pace of coalition operations against the Islamic State in Syria.[89]

- **How will the agreement be implemented?** Idlib province, the largest of the proposed de-escalation areas, has a significant Nusra Front presence. In addition, numerous other opposition fighters have been transferred to Idlib by the Syrian government following negotiated ceasefires. It is unclear how the agreement guarantors plan to extricate Nusra fighters from other armed groups in Idlib. The May 4 agreement allows for the continued targeting of Islamic State and Nusra

---

[84] "Turkey-Russia-Iran meet in Ankara for 'de-escalation zones' in Syria,"

[85] "New escalated violations witnessed by the 'de-escalation zones' with the end of the 7th day of the ceasefire agreement," Syrian Observatory for Human Rights, May 13, 2017.

[86] "Syrian opposition HNC group criticizes de-escalation deal," *Reuters*, May 5, 2017.

[87] U.S. Department of State, "Statement on Russia, Turkey, and Iran's De-Escalation Zones Plan for Syria," May 4, 2017.

[88] "Turkish forces offered truce monitoring mission in Idlib: Turkish deputy PM," *Hurriyet Daily News*, May 15, 2017.

[89] "U.S. Dismisses Russia's Ban on Aircraft Over Syrian Safe Zones," *Wall Street Journal*, May 5, 2017.

Front fighters inside the de-escalation areas. However, Russia in the past has targeted a range of Syrian opposition groups under the guise of targeting Nusra Front fighters—suggesting that oppositionists who move to de-escalation areas may be at risk.

- **How might the agreement benefit pro-government forces?** The agreement allows for guarantors to "continue the fight" against extremist groups in the de-escalation areas. If guarantors are able to dismantle extremist groups, which pose the most significant military threat to the Syrian government, it could clear the way for the elimination of the remainder of the armed opposition—if they were then concentrated in well-defined areas bordered by checkpoints. It is unclear whether the May 4 agreement is viewed by pro-regime forces as a way to protect civilians or as a way to confine the opposition within predetermined areas, freeing up Syrian military forces to retake the rest of the country.

Humanitarian Situation[90]

The humanitarian and protection needs of the Syrian population have increased in manifold ways since the start of the Syrian conflict in March 2011. Years of war have contributed to the vulnerability of millions of Syrians and led to an estimated 250,000 to 500,000 deaths since 2011. The majority of Syria's remaining population (estimated to be about 17 million in 2016) requires humanitarian and protection assistance. The United States is the largest donor of humanitarian assistance to Syria, and the 115th Congress may seek to further review U.S. funding and programs as well as address ongoing challenges, such as those associated with civilian protection.

Shifting frontlines, changeable territorial control, and high levels of violence make the provision of humanitarian assistance difficult if not impossible in some areas. an estimated 13.5 million people inside Syria, more than half the population, need assistance, including 4.5 million Syrians living in 13 besieged locations or other hard-to-reach areas controlled by Syrian government forces, opposition forces, or the Islamic State terrorist organization.[91]

Experts estimate that there are more than 6.3 million Internally Displaced Persons (IDPs) in Syria, but this number is imprecise and fluid. Many Syrians, some of whom have been displaced multiple times within the country, leave their homes to escape violence and then return when conflict in their area decreases. It is not clear how many IDPs are affected by repeat displacements, or if, or how often, they are included in IDP counts. Many IDPs stay in unofficial shelters, unfinished buildings, makeshift accommodations, and unofficial camps. IDPs are predominantly women, children, and the elderly. Syria also hosts refugees from elsewhere, and these populations have been vulnerable to the conflict, particularly Palestinian refugees. New displacements continue to occur in areas where there is fighting. According to UNOCHA, the rate of displacement in 2016 averaged 5,000 people per day.[92]

---

[90] Prepared by Rhoda Margesson, Specialist in International Humanitarian Policy.

[91] Under-Secretary-General for Humanitarian Affairs and Emergency Relief Coordinator, Stephen O'Brien, Remarks at the 'Syria–Humanitarian Assistance and Resilience' Segment of the Ministerial-level Plenary Session of the Brussels Conference on Supporting the Future of Syria and the Region, April 5, 2017. With regard to access for relief aid workers in Syria, and U.N. cross-border and cross-line delivery of humanitarian aid to conflict affected areas without the Syrian Arab Republic Government's approval, see relevant Security Council Resolutions, including 2139 (2014), 2165 (2014), 2191 (2014), and 2258 (2015), 2332 (2016) and 2286 (2016) and Reports of the Secretary-General on the Implementation of Security Council Resolutions.

[92] UNOCHA, *Syrian Arab Republic: Humanitarian Needs Overview 2017,* December 2016; Under-Secretary-General for Humanitarian Affairs and Emergency Relief Coordinator, Stephen O'Brien, Remarks at the 'Syria–Humanitarian (continued...)

In addition, according to the U.N. High Commissioner for Refugees (UNHCR), more than 5 million Syrians have registered as refugees abroad, with most fleeing to countries in the immediate surrounding region (Turkey, Lebanon, Jordan, Iraq, and Egypt) as well as Europe, where 1.2 million Syrians have applied for asylum.[93] Experts recognize that some fleeing Syrians have not registered as refugees and have chosen instead to blend in with the local population, living in rented accommodations and makeshift shelters, particularly in towns and cities. UNOCHA estimates that 85% of all Syrian refugees are living outside camps in mostly urban settings, where refugees are often more difficult to identify and assist.[94]

National and international humanitarian efforts have been severely constrained in providing assistance and protection to IDPs and others affected by the conflict in Syria due to restrictions imposed by the parties to the conflict. Government and opposition interference, the closure of key border points, bureaucratic procedures, and resource shortfalls continue to hinder aid delivery, particularly to those living in besieged and hard-to-reach areas.[95] Beyond the security situation for aid convoys, the United Nations also has reported on the challenges of procuring the necessary permits from the Syrian government to deliver aid to several areas it is otherwise ready to reach.

International Humanitarian Funding

In December 2016, the United Nations, along with humanitarian partners, launched several 2017 appeals, including the Syria Regional Refugee and Resilience Plan (3RP) for $5.6 billion and the Humanitarian Response Plan (HRP) for Syria for $3.4 billion. Since 2011, U.N. appeals have consistently remained underfunded and have resulted in cuts to food aid and cash assistance. According to UNHCR, chronic funding shortages greatly limit aid programs for refugees and host communities in the region.

As of May 24, 2017, the 3RP appeal was 34.5% funded and the appeal for Syria was 20% funded.[96] Despite multiyear donor pledges of $3.73 billion made at the 2016 London conference and possible loan options from international financial institutions that could widen the resource base, funding remains insufficient for immediate needs.[97] In March 2017, donors pledged a combined $6 billion for humanitarian programs in 2017 and $3.7 billion for 2018.[98]

(...continued)

Assistance and Resilience' Segment of the Ministerial-level Plenary Session of the Brussels Conference on Supporting the Future of Syria and the Region, April 5, 2017.

[93] U.N. High Commissioner for Refugees (UNHCR), "Syria Regional Refugee Response Portal" at: http://data.unhcr.org/syrianrefugees/regional.php; and UNHCR, "Mediterranean Situation," Operational Portal Refugee Situations at: http://data2.unhcr.org/en/situations/mediterranean. See also UNOCHA, *Syria Regional Refugee Response Inter-agency Information Sharing Portal*, April 5, 2017; International Organization for Migration (IOM), "Irregular Migrant, Refugee Arrivals in Europe Top One Million in 2015," December 22, 2015; and "Mediterranean Migrant Arrivals Top 363,348 in 2016; Deaths at Sea: 5,079," January 6, 2017.

[94] UNOCHA, *Syrian Arab Republic: Humanitarian Needs Overview 2017*, December 2016.

[95] Under-Secretary-General for Humanitarian Affairs and Emergency Relief Coordinator, Stephen O'Brien, Remarks at the 'Syria–Humanitarian Assistance and Resilience' Segment of the Ministerial-level Plenary Session of the Brussels Conference on Supporting the Future of Syria and the Region, April 5, 2017.

[96] In the final tally by UNOCHA's Financial Tracking Service, the 2016 3RP was 60% funded and the HRP for Syria was 49% funded.

[97] For post-conference financial tracking, see https://2c8kkt1ykog81j8k9p47oglb-wpengine.netdna-ssl.com/wp-content/uploads/2016/11/Final-Syria-Report-Sept-16.pdf.

[98] U.N. News Center, "Donors Pledge $6 Billion to Help Support Future of War-Torn Syria at UN-Backed Conference," April 5, 2017.

U.S. Humanitarian Assistance

The United States is the largest donor of humanitarian assistance to the Syria crisis. Since FY2012, it has allocated more than $6.5 billion to address the humanitarian impact of the Syria crisis using existing funding from global humanitarian accounts and some reprogrammed funding.[99]

In December 2016, the Further Continuing and Security Assistance Appropriations Act, 2017 (P.L. 114-254), made funds available at FY2016 levels primarily through the Migration and Refugee Assistance (MRA) and International Disaster Assistance (IDA) accounts. Division B of the Act provided an additional $916 million in FY2017 supplemental funding through MRA and IDA for the humanitarian response in Iraq and Syria. The Consolidated Appropriations Act, 2017 (P.L. 115-31) provides funding to several global humanitarian accounts, including $3.058 billion in MRA and $3.811 billion in IDA, some of which will be used to respond to the Iraq-Syria crises.

The Trump Administration's FY2018 appropriations request seeks more than $2.5 billion in enduring and OCO funding for the IDA account, some of which would be used to respond to the Iraq and Syria crises. The Administration also seeks more than $2.7 billion for the MRA account, including $1.2 billion for MRA-funded programs in the Near East region.

In the December 2016 continuing resolution, $1 billion in Economic Support Funds-OCO (ESF-OCO) was appropriated for stabilization and community support in Syria, some of which may be used for humanitarian activities.

In the FY2017 Consolidated Appropriations Act, a Relief and Recovery Fund, established under Section 8004, using ESF, INCLE, Peacekeeping, and FMF accounts provides $169 million for Iraq and Syria on a range of activities, some of which could be considered humanitarian. None of these figures include emergency food aid appropriated to the Food for Peace program (P.L. 480, Title II). Country allocations of funds appropriated in the FY2017 omnibus (P.L. 115-31) will be determined through consultations between Congress and the executive branch.[100]

For additional details on the humanitarian situation in Syria, see CRS In Focus IF10648, *Syria's Humanitarian and Protection Crisis: Current Status*, by Rhoda Margesson.

U.S. Policy and Assistance

Perceived Threats and Challenges for Policymakers

Syria's descent into chaotic conflict over the past six years has generated several interrelated threats to U.S. national security and challenges for U.S. decisionmakers. Direct threats to U.S. security and interests include the following:

---

[99] State Department Bureau of Population, Refugees, and Migration, U.S. Humanitarian Assistance in Response to the Syrian Crisis, April 5, 2017. See also USAID, *Syria–Complex Emergency*, Fact Sheet #4, Fiscal Year (FY) 2017, April 27, 2017.

[100] The Consolidated Appropriations Act, 2017 provides funding to several global humanitarian accounts, including $3.058 billion to the Migration and Refugee Assistance (MRA) account and $3.811 billion to the International Disaster Assistance (IDA) account, some of which will be used to respond to the Iraq-Syria crises.

- the rise to power in some areas of Syria of violent Islamist extremist groups, some of whom use Syria as a safe haven to plan and train for transnational terrorist attacks;

- the use of chemical weapons by Syrian government forces and non-state actors;

- the proliferation of small arms and military weaponry among a broad spectrum of Syrian non-state actors;

- the destruction of major urban areas and economic infrastructure in Syria, the resulting internal and external displacement of millions of Syrian civilians, and corresponding pressures placed on neighboring countries, refugee transit and destination countries; and

- interventions in Syria by regional and extra-regional actors, with associated effects on regional and international balances of power.

The above threats have challenged U.S. policymakers by

- complicating other diplomatic priorities, such as negotiations with Iran over its nuclear program;

- threatening to weaken global norms associated with international humanitarian law;

- straining the international humanitarian response system; and

- raising questions about the credibility and effectiveness of U.S. foreign policy commitments and international institutions, such as the United Nations Security Council.

U.S. concerns about these threats and challenges have evolved in relation to developments in the Syria conflict and changes in its international context, with executive branch officials and Members of Congress assigning different priority to different issues over time. Overall, the United States has balanced several basic objectives: securing an end to the conflict, ridding Syria of chemical weapons, and fighting violent Islamist extremist groups active in Syria.

U.S. Strategy and Policy

One central question for U.S. policy toward the Syria conflict since 2011 has been whether or not the United States should support and pursue a resolution of the conflict that would recognize a continuing role for Syrian President Bashar al Asad. Policy proposals over time have reflected various assumptions about whether Asad's continued rule or its end would bring the conflict to a close. Counterterrorism and regional stability concerns became amplified by developments in Syria's underlying conflict and arguably, in the case of the Islamic State, took precedence over U.S. concerns about Asad's future. U.S. and regional policymakers have sought to determine which problem in Syria to confront first–Asad or the Islamic State—and U.S. officials and observers have debated how different approaches and outcomes would affect Syria's short- and long-term stability.

Syria Policy Under the Obama Administration

In 2011, the Obama Administration called for Syrian President Bashar al Asad to step down amid protests in Syria inspired by the "Arab Spring." This call was based in part on concern that, if left unchallenged, the Syrian government's use of force against demonstrators would set a dangerous precedent that political violence against civilians could continue unchecked. Asad refused to leave office, and the conflict intensified. Humanitarian pressures and threats posed by terrorist groups grew.

President Barack Obama and his Administration pursued various policies to protect U.S. interests with regard to Syria, while implementing an overarching regional strategy that prioritized efforts to freeze Iran's nuclear program and reduce the direct involvement of U.S. military forces in combat operations. The Obama Administration engaged from 2012 through 2017 in multilateral efforts to reach a negotiated settlement to the conflict that would result in Asad's departure but preserve some elements of the Syrian government. This approach was informed by parallel U.S concerns about terrorism and efforts to contain and defeat violent Islamist extremist groups active in Syria, principally the Al Qaeda-affiliated Nusra Front and the Islamic State organization.

The Obama Administration sought to bolster its diplomacy and counterterrorism policy toward Syria through the provision of nonlethal U.S. support to select Syrian opposition groups, reported covert assistance to some armed groups, and overt training and lethal assistance to certain vetted Syrian forces. Obama Administration officials often asserted that there was "no military solution to the conflict." That formulation appeared to reflect the Administration's stated preference for the conflict to be brought to a close in a way that would preserve some elements of the Syrian state apparatus rather than allowing military developments to result in state collapse or the outright victory of pro-Asad forces.

As the Trump Administration has begun articulating its approach to Syria in 2017, the underlying conflict in Syria and associated counterterrorism, humanitarian, and international systemic challenges that vexed the Obama Administration have persisted. President Trump and his Administration have identified the defeat of the Islamic State organization as their highest priority in the Middle East, and President Trump directed his Administration in January to develop "a new plan to defeat ISIS."

On April 6, Secretary of State Rex Tillerson outlined the Trump Administration's vision for the sequencing of U.S. efforts, subject to developments in Syria:

> Overall, the situation in Syria is one where our approach today and our policy today is first to defeat ISIS. By defeating ISIS, we remove one of the disruptive elements in Syria that exists today. That begins to clarify, for us, opposition forces and regime forces, and working with the coalition—as you know, there is a large coalition of international players and allies who are involved in the future resolution in Syria.

> So it's to defeat ISIS; it's to begin to stabilize areas of Syria, stabilize areas in the south of Syria, stabilize areas around Raqqa, through cease-fire agreements between the Syrian regime forces and opposition forces; stabilize those areas, begin to restore some normalcy to them, restore them to local governments—and there are local leaders who are ready to return, some who've left as refugees that are ready to return, to govern these areas; use local forces that will be part of the liberation effort to develop the local security forces—law enforcement, police force; and then use other forces to create outer perimeters of security so that areas like Raqqa, areas in the south, can begin to provide a secure environment so refugees can begin to go home and begin the rebuilding process.

> In the midst of that, through the Geneva process, we will start a political process to resolve Syria's future in terms of its governance structure. And that ultimately, in our view, will lead to a resolution of Bashar al-Assad's departure.[101]

President Trump has discussed the possibility of establishing "safe zones" in Syria, but to date his Administration has not publicly defined what such an initiative might entail or signaled an intent to pursue it imminently. The April 2017 chemical weapons attack and U.S. military response appear to have complicated the Trump Administration's attempts to pursue a more cooperative relationship with the Russian government with regard to the conflict in Syria. U.S. efforts to contain or more aggressively curtail Iran's security support for its foreign partners may also affect developments in Syria.

---

[101] Secretary of State Rex Tillerson, Remarks with National Security Advisor H.R. McMaster, April 6, 2017.

Members of Congress may similarly reassess U.S. priorities and strategy in Syria and may consider a range of general and specific questions as the Trump Administration develops and seeks congressional support for its approach.

- What U.S. national security interests are at stake in Syria? How do these Syria-specific interests relate to broader U.S. regional or global interests? Which of these interests, if any, can or should be given priority? Why? What might be the consequences of prioritizing some U.S. interests over others?

- Who are the key internal and external actors in Syria? What are their relative interests and goals? How are they pursuing those interests? What opportunities and risks do these factors create for the United States?

- What short-, medium-, and long-term objectives should the United States pursue in Syria?

- What authorization might a given policy option, such as military intervention to protect civilians, have under existing domestic and international law? What implications might the pursuit of that option have for future domestic or international legal norms?

- How should various instruments of national power be used in concert to further U.S. interests? What material, financial, or reputational costs are associated with different options? How should Congress define the authorities and resources available to the executive branch to pursue U.S. policy?

- How should the United States plan and prepare for the long-term challenges and needs created by the conflict in Syria? How should Congress expect developments in Syria to affect regional and international security and corresponding demands on U.S. attention and resources over the next 10 years?

Congress has directed President Trump to transmit a report describing a strategy for Syria within 90 days of the enactment of the FY2017 Consolidated Appropriations Act (Section 10006 of Division C of P.L. 115-31, which became law May 5, 2017). In his signing statement on the act, President Trump identified this reporting requirement as a provision that would "mandate or regulate the submission of certain executive branch information to the Congress," and said, "I will treat these provisions in a manner consistent with my constitutional authority to withhold information that could impair foreign relations, national security, the deliberative processes of the executive branch, or the performance of my constitutional duties."[102]

U.S. Assistance to Syrians and the Syrian Opposition

A broad set of bilateral U.S. sanctions on Syria existed prior to the outbreak of conflict, and some, such as those triggered by Syria's designation as a state sponsor of terrorism, initially had a limiting effect on the delivery of U.S. assistance in the country. The FY2014 Consolidated Appropriations Act (Section 7041[i]) of Division K of P.L. 113-76) significantly expanded the Administration's authority to provide nonlethal assistance in Syria for certain purposes using the Economic Support Fund (ESF) account. Such assistance had been restricted by a series of preexisting provisions of law (including some terrorism-related sanctions provisions) that required the President to assert emergency and contingency authorities (i.e., Sections 451 and 614 of the Foreign Assistance Act of 1961, as amended) to provide such assistance to the unarmed

---

[102] President George W. Bush included this formulation in 10 signing statements from 2003 to 2006.

Syrian opposition and communities in Syria. Such assistance has been provided to select unarmed opposition groups on a periodic basis since May 2012, although the Administration has not publicly released a detailed accounting or list of recipients. Congressional committees of jurisdiction are notified when the Administration intends to obligate funds for these purposes.

The FY2014 assistance authorities, as expanded and extended by the FY2015 Appropriations Act (Section 7041[h] of P.L. 113-235), made FY2015 and prior year ESF funding available "notwithstanding any other provision of law" for select nonlethal purposes. The FY2016 Appropriations Act (Section 7041[h] of P.L. 114-113) extended this authority further, granting notwithstanding exceptions for FY2016 ESF funds as well as for FY2016 funds in the International Narcotics Control and Law Enforcement (INCLE) and Peacekeeping Operations (PKO) accounts. The Obama Administration used the INCLE and PKO accounts to support justice sector activities in opposition-held areas of Syria and to provide nonlethal assistance to select armed opposition groups.

The FY2017 Consolidated Appropriations Act (Section 7041[j] of Division J of P.L. 115-31) amended and expanded the categories of assistance authorized in FY2016 (changes *italicized* below) to include "non-lethal assistance for programs to address the needs of civilians affected by conflict in Syria, and for programs that seek to—

> (A) establish governance in Syria that is representative, inclusive, and accountable;
>
> (B) *empower women through political and economic programs, and address the psychosocial needs of women and their families in Syria and neighboring countries*;
>
> (C) develop and implement political processes that are democratic, transparent, and adhere to the rule of law;
>
> (D) further the legitimacy *and viability* of the Syrian opposition through cross-border programs;
>
> (E) develop *and sustain* civil society and independent media in Syria;
>
> (F) promote *stability and* economic development in Syria;
>
> (G) document, investigate, and prosecute human rights violations in Syria, including through transitional justice programs and support for nongovernmental organizations;
>
> (H) *expand the role of women in negotiations to end the violence and in any political transition in Syria*;
>
> (I) assist Syrian refugees whose education has been interrupted by the ongoing conflict to complete higher education requirements *at universities and other academic institutions in the region, and through distance learning;*
>
> (J) assist vulnerable populations in Syria and in neighboring countries;
>
> (K) *protect and preserve the cultural identity of the people of Syria as a counterbalance to extremism, particularly those living in neighboring countries and among youth;*
>
> (L) *protect and preserve cultural heritage sites in Syria, particularly those damaged and destroyed by extremists; and*
>
> (M) *counter extremism in Syria.*

The FY2017 act requires the Secretary of State to "take all *practicable* steps to ensure that mechanisms are in place for the adequate monitoring, oversight, and control of such assistance inside Syria," and requires the Secretary of State to "promptly inform the appropriate congressional committees of each significant instance in which assistance provided pursuant to this subsection has been *diverted or destroyed*, to include the type and amount of assistance, a description of the incident and parties involved, and an explanation of the response of the Department of State."

The act further requires the Trump Administration to update a previously required comprehensive interagency strategy prior to using the authorities. That strategy must include a "mission statement, achievable objectives and timelines, and a description of inter-agency and donor coordination and implementation of such strategy." The strategy, which may be classified, must also include "a description of oversight and vetting procedures to prevent the misuse of funds." All funds obligated pursuant to the authorities are subject to established congressional notification procedures.

The U.S. Syria Transition Assistance and Response Team operates from Turkey and coordinates U.S. assistance to Syria, including assistance to opposition held areas. The State Department requested more than $480 million in FY2016 and FY2017 funding to provide nonlethal support to vetted, moderate armed opposition groups, other opposition actors, and communities in opposition-held areas of Syria. Section 7041(j) of Division J of the Consolidated Appropriations Act, 2017, allows certain accounts to fund "non-lethal assistance for programs to address the needs of civilians affected by conflict in Syria" for select purposes.

The Trump Administration has requested $191.5 million in Overseas Contingency Operation funding for State Department-administered programs in Syria for FY2018, including $150 million in Economic Support and Development Fund-OCO monies.

Nonlethal Assistance to Armed Syrian Opposition Elements

Until the creation of the Syria Train and Equip program in 2014 discussed below, overt U.S. assistance to armed opposition forces remained restricted to nonlethal items. Prior to the creation of the program and the extension of the FY2016 foreign assistance authorities discussed above, congressional appropriators and authorizers had not provided the Administration with notwithstanding authority to provide nonlethal assistance to armed opposition groups. For that purpose, the Obama Administration had relied upon special authorities granted by the Foreign Assistance Act of 1961, as amended (Section 552[c] and Section 614).

In 2012, the Administration began to use these special authorities to provide food rations and medical supplies to the National Coalition of Revolutionary and Opposition Forces (SOC) and the Turkey-based Syrian Military Council (SMC). Since then, U.S. assistance has expanded to encompass a range of smaller, local groups. In August 2015, the State Department reported

> Non-lethal assistance is being provided to a range of civilian opposition groups, including local councils, civil society organizations, and SOC-affiliated entities to bolster their institutional capacity, create linkages among opposition groups inside and outside Syria, and help counter violent extremism. These efforts enable the delivery of basic goods and essential services to liberated communities as they step in to fill voids in local governance. In addition to civil administration training programs, we have provided opposition groups with a wide array of critical equipment, including generators, ambulances, cranes, dump trucks, fire trucks, water storage units, search and rescue equipment, educational kits for schools, winterization materials, and commodity baskets for needy families in the local community.[103]

This equipment is used to bolster governance by providing services such as emergency power, sanitation, water, and education services. Other U.S. assistance provided under authorities granted

---

[103] Office of the State Department Spokesperson, "Syrian Crisis: U.S. Efforts and Assistance," August 7, 2015.

by Congress in FY2014-FY2016 appropriations acts and the FY2017 continuing resolution supports the maintenance of public safety, rule of law, and the documentation of human rights violations.

Obama Administration officials noted that U.S. efforts to deliver and monitor security assistance and other aid inside Syria have been hindered by border closures, ongoing fighting, and risks from extremist groups. Some U.S. nonlethal assistance to armed opposition groups has fallen into the hands of unintended recipients and has led to changes in delivery and oversight mechanisms.[104] Infighting among some opposition forces, the empowerment of the Islamic State in Syria, and concerns expressed by other outside actors such as Russia and Turkey have created further complications. Although the Islamic State has lost control of border crossings it formerly held, other anti-U.S. extremist groups control some border crossings in northwestern Syria. As such, access issues may continue to hinder efforts to expand support to anti-IS forces.

In July 2016, the Government Accountability Office released a report examining the delivery of nonlethal assistance to Syria. The report recommended that the Department of State, USAID, and their implementing partners incorporate greater oversight of fraud risk in the delivery of such aid.[105]

Syria Train and Equip Program[106]

Congress authorized and funded a train and equip program for vetted Syrians in 2014 for select purposes, including supporting U.S. efforts to combat the Islamic State and other terrorist organizations in Syria and promoting the conditions for a negotiated settlement to Syria's civil war (Section 1209 of H.R. 3979, P.L. 113-291). The program's limited results as of September 2015, Russian military intervention in Syria, and support by some Members of Congress for broader civilian protection missions led the Obama Administration to alter the program beginning in October 2015. Obama Administration officials described their intended overall approach to the redesigned program as "transactional" and performance-based, with Syrian beneficiaries receiving U.S. support as opportunities presented themselves and relative to their effectiveness on the battlefield and the alignment of their actions with U.S. interests.

The revamped train and equip program has since shifted away from training and equipping "New Syrian Force" units of vetted new recruits and toward "equipping and enabling ...a select group of vetted leaders and their units" inside Syria who are fighting the Islamic State organization. Trained and equipped individuals fight under the rubric of a Kurdish-Arab coalition force in northern Syria known as the Syrian Democratic Forces (SDF) and a force known as the "New Syrian Army" (NSA) in the southeast. Equipment, including some weaponry and ammunition, has been provided to SDF and NSA forces, and U.S. special operations personnel have been deployed to Syria to advise and assist the SDF in operations against the Islamic State.

The shift from training and equipping of new vetted units toward equipping existing vetted armed groups has featured some unique risks. While equipment losses have not proven to be a major systemic concern since the change was announced, some Syrian opposition groups that reportedly

---

[104] Opposition infighting in late 2013 led to the capture of some nonlethal U.S. assistance by Islamist groups. U.S. officials subsequently revisited some delivery and monitoring mechanisms and worked to improve the reliability and security of delivery channels. Dasha Afanasieva and Humeyra Pamuk, "U.S., Britain suspend aid to north Syria after Islamists seize weapons store," Reuters, December 11, 2013.

[105] *Syria Humanitarian Assistance*, Government Accountability Office, July 2016.

[106] For background on the origins of this program and related legislation, see CRS Report R43727, *Train and Equip Program for Syria: Authorities, Funding, and Issues for Congress*, by Christopher M. Blanchard and Amy Belasco.

have received U.S. equipment and weaponry have surrendered or lost these items to other groups, including to the Islamic State.[107] The comprehensive training approach under the program's first iteration sought to create unit cohesion, groom and support reliable leaders to serve as U.S. partners, and inculcate a spirit of nationalist motivation among fighters in the place of local, sectarian, or ideological goals. The amended approach appears to have more rapidly and effectively equipped some anti-IS forces in some areas of Syria, but may have fewer direct effects on the internal development and practices of forces, some of whom may influence security in Syria for years to come. Increased reliance on vetted group leaders may also have reduced direct U.S. visibility and influence over which individual fighters receive U.S.-origin weapons or how U.S.-origin equipment is managed and secured.

Related Appropriations and Authorities

The underlying authority for the Department of Defense Syria train and equip program remains Section 1209 of the FY2015 defense authorization act (P.L. 113-291), as amended and extended by subsequent legislation. Congress has not appropriated funds specifically for the Syria train and equip program since the program's inception. Congress has authorized the reprogramming of funds by the Department of Defense to operations and maintenance accounts to fund program activities, subject to the prior approval of the congressional defense committees. In total, as of May 2017 Congress had reviewed and approved Defense Department requests to reprogram more than $1.25 billion in monies from other accounts for the program since 2014.[108]

Funding transfers to operations and maintenance accounts for Syria train and equip program activities remain subject to the prior approval of congressional defense and appropriations committees pursuant to the terms of the FY2017 NDAA (P.L. 114-328), which extended the authorization for the program through December 31, 2018. President Obama requested $250 million for the Syria train and equip program for FY2017, and in March 2017, the Trump Administration requested an additional $180 million in FY2017 funds for the program.

As noted above, the FY2017 Consolidated Appropriations Act (Division C of P.L. 115-31) provides $980 million for a Counter-ISIL Train and Equip Fund available until September 30, 2018. The act also makes available an additional $626.4 million for the fund that would provide funding requested by President Trump. These additional funds cannot be obligated or expended until 15 days after the President submits a required report "on the United States strategy for the defeat" of the Islamic State organization (Section 10005 of Division C of P.L. 115-31).

The Trump Administration has requested $500 million for Syria train and equip program efforts as part of its FY2018 defense appropriations request for the Counter-IS Train and Equip Fund.

---

[107] The program came under intense scrutiny in the wake of August and September 2015 reports that some of the small number of U.S. trainees that had completed the program quit and others may have turned over equipment and weaponry to Jabhat al Nusra, the Al Qaeda affiliate that controls much of Idlib Province in northwest Syria. As of October 2015, U.S. officials reported that the program had produced 124 graduates, 70 of whom had returned to Syria in September 2015. Of the other 54, U.S. CENTCOM Commander General Lloyd Austin told the Senate Armed Services Committee that "four or five" then remained "in the fight" against the Islamic State in Syria, after having come under Jabhat al Nusra attack in July 2015.

[108] Prior approval reprogramming request notifications can be reviewed on the website of the Office of the Under Secretary of Defense (Comptroller) under Budget Execution materials for corresponding fiscal years.

Table 1. Syria Train and Equip Program: Appropriations Actions and Requests

$, thousands

	FY2015 Approved Transfers	FY2016 Approved Transfers	FY2017 Approved Transfers	FY2017 Requests	FY2018 Syria-Specific Request
	225,000 (O&M FY15)	116,453 (CTPF FY15/16)	50,000 (CTPF FY16/17)	430,000	500,000 (CTEF)
	220,500 (CTPF FY15/16)	300,000 (CTPF FY16/17)	220,000 (CTPF FY17/17)		
	279,500 (CTPF FY15/16)	-	-		
	-157,408 (CTPF FY15/16)	-	-		
Net Total	**567,592**	**416,453**	**270,000**	**430,000**	**500,000**

Source: Executive branch appropriations requests and reprogramming notifications.

Notes: Counterterrorism Partnerships Fund (CTPF). Counter-Islamic State of Iraq and Syria (ISIS) Train and Equip Fund (CTEF). The authority for the Syria Train and Equip Program requires the Department of Defense to submit prior approval notices to transfer funds into various service and department-wide Operations and Maintenance accounts for program activities. Funds listed were approved for transfer by the required congressional defense and appropriations committees during the fiscal years noted.

Proposed Restrictions on Man-Portable Air Defense Systems (MANPADS)

Since 2013, Congress has considered and enacted some proposals to restrict or govern the use of authorized and appropriated funds for the procurement or transfer of man-portable air defense systems (MANPADS) to Syria. Proposed MANPADS restrictions have reflected the concerns of some Members of Congress that MANPADS could fall into the hands of hostile parties and threaten civilian aircraft, allied military aircraft, and U.S. aircraft that are conducting air strikes against terrorist groups or that may otherwise be supporting Syrian groups.

In the 113th Congress, proposals sought to define the types of assistance that could be provided and to place conditions or restrictions on the transfer of certain weapons systems to Syrians (S. 960, H.R. 1327). Section 9016 of the FY2015 defense appropriations act (P.L. 113-235) stated that none of the funds used pursuant to the authorities contained in the section for the Syria Train and Equip program "shall be used for the procurement or transfer of man portable air defense systems."[109] Parallel authority for the program was established by Section 1209 of the FY2015 defense authorization act (P.L. 113-291) and extended until December 31, 2018, by the FY2017 NDAA. The Section 1209 authority, as subsequently amended, does not restrict the purchase or transfer of MANPADS pursuant to the authority.

In the 114th Congress, for FY2016, the House-proposed version of the FY2016 defense appropriations act (H.R. 2685) would have authorized and appropriated monies for the continuation of the Syria Train and Equip program and was amended to provide that "none of the funds used pursuant to this authority shall be used for the procurement or transfer of man-portable air-defense systems."[110] As enacted, the final version of the FY2016 defense appropriations act (Division C of P.L. 114-113) did not include a Syria-related prohibition on MANPADS procurement or transfer, but provided in Section 9013 that "none of the funds made available by this Act under the heading 'Iraq Train and Equip Fund' may be used to procure or transfer man-portable air defense systems." The 114th Congress considered and the House adopted a proposal for FY2017 that would have prohibited the use of certain funds made available by the act to procure or transfer MANPADS (Section 9013 of the House-passed version of the FY2017 defense

---

[109] In June 2014, the House adopted H.Amdt. 914 to H.R. 4870, which provided that "None of the funds made available by this Act may be obligated or expended to transfer man-portable air defense systems (MANPADS) to any entity in Syria." It was included in the House engrossed version of the bill as Section 10010.

[110] H.Amdt. 487 to H.R. 2685.

appropriations act [H.R. 5293]). The House further adopted an *en bloc* floor amendment during its consideration of the FY2017 defense authorization bill (incorporated as Section 1229 of H.R. 4909) that included an amendment to prohibit the obligation or expenditure of funds authorized to be appropriated for or otherwise available to the Department of Defense for FY2017 "to transfer or facilitate the transfer" of MANPADS to any entity in Syria.[111] The Senate-passed versions of the FY2017 defense authorization (S. 2943) and the FY2017 defense appropriation (S. 3000) did not contain similar provisions.

Section 1224 of the FY2017 NDAA provides that funds available to the Department of Defense for FY2017 may not be used to provide MANPADS to vetted Syrian opposition forces until the Secretary of Defense and the Secretary of State jointly submit a report on the determination and 30 days elapse after the date of the report submittal.

In the 115th Congress, the FY2017 Consolidated Appropriations Act (§9013 of Division C of P.L. 115-31) prohibits the use of funds made available by the act for the Counter-ISIL Train and Equip Fund to procure or transfer MANPADs.

In 2016, some media reports suggested that non-U.S. entities sought to provide MANPADS to entities in Syria as a means of responding to escalating violence against opposition-held areas and empowering certain anti-Asad forces to defend themselves and Syrian civilians from air assaults by Syrian government and Russian air forces.[112] Responding to questions about the potential provision of MANPADS to Syrian rebels by Gulf states, State Department Deputy Spokesman Mark Toner stated, "We cannot dictate what other countries—and I'm not naming names—... may or may not decide to do in terms of supporting certain groups within Syria."[113] Press reports since 2012 have documented the appearance of MANPADS in limited numbers among some Syrian armed groups.[114]

Other Reported U.S. Assistance

Then-Secretary of Defense Chuck Hagel said in a September 2013 hearing before the Senate Foreign Relations Committee that the Obama Administration was taking steps to provide arms to some Syrian rebels under covert action authorities.[115] Several press accounts citing unnamed U.S. government sources subsequently described details of reported U.S. and partner nation efforts to that effect.[116] To date, other U.S. officials have not publicly acknowledged any such efforts or publicly described which elements of the Syrian opposition may have received U.S. training or support via any such channels, what any training may have entailed, what types of weaponry may have been provided, or what safeguards may be in place to monitor the disposition of equipment and the actions of any U.S.-trained or equipped personnel. One June 2015 article discussed differences of opinion among Members of Congress about future funding for the reported

---

[111] See Amendment 81 in H.Rept. 114-571, adopted as part of en bloc amendment H.Amdt. 1046 to H.R. 4909. If enacted, the amendment would provide that, "none of the funds authorized to be appropriated by this Act or otherwise made available for the Department of Defense for fiscal year 2017 may be obligated or expended to transfer or facilitate the transfer of man-portable air defense systems (MANPADS) to any entity in Syria."

[112] Jonathan Landay and Arshad Mohammed, "Gulf may arm rebels now Syria truce is dead - U.S. officials," September 27, 2016.

[113] State Department press briefing by Deputy Spokesperson Mark C. Toner, September 27, 2016.

[114] "Syrian Rebels Get Missiles," *Wall Street Journal*, October 17, 2012; "Officials: Syrian rebels' arsenal includes up to 40 antiaircraft missile systems," *Washington Post*, November 28, 2012; "As Russian planes bombard Syrian rebels, debate over anti-aircraft missiles returns," *Los Angeles Times*, May 1, 2016.

[115] Secretary Hagel said, "it was June of this year that the president made the decision to support lethal assistance to the opposition. As you all know, we have been very supportive with hundreds of millions of dollars of nonlethal assistance. The vetting process that Secretary Kerry noted has been significant, but—I'll ask General Dempsey if he wants to add anything—but we, the Department of Defense, have not been directly involved in this. This is, as you know, a covert action. And, as Secretary Kerry noted, probably to [go] into much more detail would—would require a closed or classified hearing."

[116] Adam Entous, Julian E. Barnes and Siobhan Gorman, "U.S. Begins Shipping Arms for Syrian Rebels," *Wall Street Journal*, June 26, 2013; Greg Miller, "CIA ramping up covert training program for moderate Syrian rebels," *Washington Post*, October 2, 2013; Greg Miller and Karen DeYoung, "Secret CIA effort in Syria faces large funding cut," *Washington Post*, June 12, 2015.

program.[117] In October 2015, unnamed U.S. officials were cited in press reports that suggested that Russia was actively targeting Syrian opposition groups that had received covert support from the United States.[118]

U.S.-Origin Weaponry and the Syria Conflict

From 2014 onward, various anti-Asad forces released videos of their operatives loading and firing what appeared to be U.S.-origin antitank weaponry in Syria.[119] In April 2014, an official affiliated with the now-defunct opposition group Harakat Hazm told the *New York Times* that "friendly states" had provided "modest numbers" of the weapons.[120] The commander of the group told the *Washington Post* that those who supplied the missiles had U.S. government approval and said the shipment suggested "a change in the U.S. attitude toward allowing Syria's friends to support the Syrian people."[121]

Asked in April 2014 about the reported shipments and use of U.S. origin weaponry by Syrian rebels, U.S. National Security Council spokeswoman Bernadette Meehan said, "The United States is committed to building the capacity of the moderate opposition, including through the provision of assistance to vetted members of the moderate armed opposition. As we have consistently said, we are not going to detail every single type of our assistance."[122] In May 2014, an unnamed senior Administration official reiterated that formulation to members of the press in a background briefing, while stating that "asymmetry which exists on the ground militarily, unfortunately, between the regime and the moderate opposition is problematic for the emergence of the kinds of political conditions necessary for a serious political process. And we and others are focused on that."[123]

Specific public information is lacking about the sources of U.S.-origin weaponry and which units or personnel may have continuing access to U.S.-origin weaponry.[124] In 2015, a range of opposition groups largely affiliated with the Free Syrian Army movement published videos that purported to depict their personnel firing U.S.-origin antitank weapons. This includes groups targeted by Russian air strikes, some of whom have subsequently posted footage of their fighters using such weaponry to repel follow-on ground attacks by pro-Asad forces.[125] Islamist groups also have posted similar videos and images of captured U.S.-origin antitank weapon stocks, including the Ansar al Islam Front,[126] Jabhat al Nusra,[127] and the Islamic State.[128]

---

[117] Miller and DeYoung, "Secret CIA effort in Syria faces large funding cut," *Washington Post*, June 12, 2015.

[118] Adam Entous, "U.S. Sees Russian Drive Against CIA-Backed Rebels in Syria," *Wall Street Journal*, October 5, 2015.

[119] See Harakat Hazm YouTube Channel, April 15, 2014, at http://www.youtube.com/watch?v=5x5Q4aTGvu0.

[120] Ben Hubbard, "Syrian Election Announced; Rebels Report New Weapons," *New York Times*, April 21, 2014.

[121] Liz Sly, "Syrian rebels who received first U.S. missiles of war see shipment as 'an important first step,'" *Washington Post*, April 27, 2014.

[122] Tom Bowman and Alice Fordham, "CIA Is Quietly Ramping Up Aid To Syrian Rebels, Sources Say," National Public Radio (Online), April 23, 2014

[123] Transcript of Background Briefing on Syria by Senior Administration Official, U.S. State Department, May 5, 2014.

[124] Section 3(a)(2) of the Arms Export Control Act (22 U.S.C. 2753 (a)(2)) applies obligations, restrictions, and possible penalties for misuse of U.S.-origin equipment to any retransfer by foreign recipients of U.S.-supplied defense articles, defense services, and related technical data to another nation. If such a retransfer occurred in the absence of prior U.S. approval, then the nation making such a transfer could be determined to be in violation of its agreement with the United States not to take such an action without prior consent from the U.S. government.

[125] See Tajammu al Izza YouTube Channel, October 1, 2015, at https://www.youtube.com/watch?v=AqGuUbVtGl8.

[126] See Ansar al Islam Front YouTube Channel, August 10, 2014, at http://www.youtube.com/watch?v=k9pxIFUKEZg and http://www.youtube.com/watch?v=1QclDMPQkPw.

[127] Umberto Bacchi, "Syria: al-Qaeda Nusra Front Shows Off Huge Cache of US Weapons Seized from Moderate Harakat Hazm Rebels," *International Business Times*, March 4, 2015; Michael Smallwood, "Captured TOW 2A Missiles Employed in Syria," *Armament Research Services*, 2015.

[128] OSC Report TRR2015062676424947, *ISIL Deploys Apparent TOW Missile System Against Regime Forces in Al Hasakah*, June 26, 2015.

> In June 2016, a joint investigation by the *New York Times* and *Al Jazeera* concluded that weapons shipped into Jordan by U.S. and Saudi intelligence services intended for Syrian rebels were instead diverted by Jordanian intelligence officials and sold on the black market.[129]

Chemical Weapons and Disarmament[130]

A major policy concern of the United States has been the use or loss of control of chemical weapons in Syria during the ongoing civil war. The reported use of the nerve agent sarin by aerial bombardment on April 4, 2017, in the town of Khan Sheikhoun in rebel-held Idlib province killed an estimated 80 to 100 people and returned the issue of chemical weapons in Syria to center stage. Secretary of State Tillerson said that the U.S. government had a "very high level of confidence" that the Syrian air force had used the nerve agent sarin in three recent attacks—on March 25, March 30, and April 4.[131] In testimony to the Senate Select Committee on Intelligence on May 11, Director of National Intelligence Daniel Coats said that Syria was probably "willing and able" to use chemical weapons again.[132]

On April 6, the United States responded with missile strikes against Al Shayrat air base which Pentagon officials stated is used to store chemical weapons.[133] President Trump said that "It is in the vital national security interest of the United States to prevent and deter the spread and use of deadly chemical weapons."[134] Secretary of State Rex Tillerson also said the U.S. strike was aimed at reestablishing the norm against chemical weapons use:

> As Assad has continued to use chemical weapons in these attacks with no response—no response from the international community—that he, in effect, is normalizing the use of chemical weapons, which may then be adopted by others. So it's important that some action be taken on behalf of the international community to make clear that the use of chemical weapons continues to be a violation of international norms.[135]

The World Health Organization said on April 5 that it was alarmed by the use of chemicals in Syria the previous day.[136] The Turkish Ministry of Health said on April 6 that it had assessed that victims of the attack were exposed to sarin.[137] The Organization for the Prohibition of Chemical Weapons (OPCW) began a Fact-Finding Mission on April 5 to investigate the event, and its inspectors collected samples which were sent to predesignated laboratories. The OPCW Director General said on April 19 that four of its laboratories had "incontrovertible" evidence that sarin or a sarin-like agent was used on April 4:

---

[129] "C.I.A. Arms for Syrian Rebels Supplied Black Market, Officials Say," *New York Times*, June 26, 2016.

[130] Prepared by Mary Beth Nikitin, Specialist in Nonproliferation.

[131] The Syrian government in 2013 joined the Chemical Weapons Convention (CWC), which bans the use of any toxic chemicals in warfare and requires—along with U.N. Security Council resolutions—that Syria destroy all of its chemical weapons stocks and production facilities under international supervision.

[132] Hearing on Worldwide Threats, Senate Select Committee on Intelligence, May 11, 2017.

[133] "Trump Orders Missile Attack in Retaliation for Syrian Chemical Strikes," *DoD News*, April 6, 2017.

[134] Statement by President Trump on Syria, April 6, 2017.

[135] Rex Tillerson, Secretary of State, Remarks with National Security Advior H.R. McMaster, April 6, 2017.

[136] World Health Organization, "WHO Alarmed by Use of Highly Toxic Chemicals in Syria," press release, April 5, 2017.

[137] Some victims of the attack were moved to Turkey for treatment, where experts could assess their symptoms and likely causes. Louisa Loveluck, "Deadly Nerve Agent Sarin Used in Deadly Attack," *Washington Post,* April 6, 2017.

> The bio-medical samples collected from three victims during their autopsy were analysed at two OPCW designated laboratories. The results of the analysis indicate that the victims were exposed to Sarin or a Sarin-like substance. Bio-medical samples from seven individuals undergoing treatment at hospitals were also analysed in two other OPCW designated laboratories. Similarly, the results of these analyses indicate exposure to Sarin or a Sarin-like substance.[138]

The largest-scale use of chemical weapons in Syria to date was an August 21, 2013, nerve gas attack, which the U.S. government estimated killed over 1,400 people.[139] In August 2013, the Obama Administration had threatened military action against Syria in response to alleged nerve gas attacks by Syrian government forces. As part of a diplomatic solution to the crisis based on a U.S.-Russian joint proposal, the Administration withdrew the threat of military force and Syria agreed to give up its chemical weapons and join the Chemical Weapons Convention (CWC). U.N. Security Council Resolution 2118 (2013) further mandated that Syria give up all its chemical weapons under Chapter VII provisions of the U.N. Charter.[140]

After joining the CWC, Syria declared that it possessed 1,300 metric tons of chemical warfare agents and precursor chemicals, including several hundred metric tons of the nerve agents sarin and VX, as well as mustard agent in ready-to-use form. The nerve agents were stored as two separate components that are combined before use, a form that facilitated removal and destruction efforts. The international community oversaw the removal and destruction of the declared chemical weapons agents from Syria, and, as of January 4, 2016, all declared Category 1 and 2 chemicals had been destroyed.[141]

The destruction of chemical weapons facilities is still underway.[142] Press reports, nongovernment experts and U.S. officials have said that the Asad regime used undeclared stocks of nerve agent in the April 4 attack in violation of its commitments under the CWC.[143] For years, the United States, the OPCW Director General and other governments have raised questions over whether Syria declared all of its chemical weapons stocks. The Organization for the Prohibition of Chemical Weapons (OPCW) has not been able to verify the completeness of the declaration, part of Syria's obligations under the CWC. The OPCW's Declaration Assessment Team (DAT) continues to investigate "gaps, inconsistencies and discrepancies" through interviews and lab analysis of samples from site visits but the cooperation of the Syrian government has been limited and little progress has been made according to OPCW Executive Council reports.[144]

---

[138] "OPCW Director-General Shares Incontrovertible Laboratory Results Concluding Exposure to Sarin," OPCW Press Release, April 19, 2017.

[139] White House Office of the Press Secretary, *Government Assessment of the Syrian Government's Use of Chemical Weapons on August 21, 2013*, August 30, 2013.

[140] Chapter VII of the U.N. Charter authorizes the use of punitive measures such as sanctions or military force.

[141] Organization for the Prohibition of Chemical Weapons, "Destruction of Syrian Chemical Weapons Completed," press release, January 4, 2016.

[142] "Note by the Director General: Progress in the Elimination of the Syrian Chemical Weapons Programme," EC-83/DG.6, August 22, 2016, https://www.opcw.org/fileadmin/OPCW/EC/83/en/ec83dg06_e_.pdf. As of August 22, 2016, the OPCW reported that 24 of the 27 declared chemical weapons production facilities (CWPFs) had been destroyed. The "poor security situation" prevents destruction of the remaining aircraft hangar and two stationary above-ground facilities. The OPCW said that Syrian government is cooperating on this matter.

[143] Joint News Conference with Secretary Mattis and Minister of Defense Lieberman in Tel Aviv, Israel, Department of Defense News Transcript, April 21, 2017; Julian E. Barnes and Maria Abi-Habib, "Syrian Attack Defies 2013 Chemical-Weapons Deal," *Wall Street Journal*, April 6, 2017.

[144] Ibid.

Since the August 2013 attack, reports of chemical weapons use in Syria have consisted primarily of accusations of chlorine use in barrel bombs until the alleged sarin use in the spring of 2017.[145] Reports of the use of chlorine gas as a chemical weapon began to surface in April 2014. The OPCW established a fact-finding mission to investigate these allegations. The use of chlorine as a weapon is banned under the Chemical Weapons Convention. Several governments—including the governments of Syria and the United States—have submitted allegations of chemical attacks to the U.N. Secretary-General and/or the OPCW.[146] The United States, the United Nations,[147] and others have assessed that the Syrian government has used chemical weapons repeatedly against opposition forces and civilians in the country. Expert teams affiliated with the U.N.-OPCW Joint Mission to Investigate Allegations of the Use of Chemical Weapons in the Syrian Arab Republic and the OPCW Fact Finding Mission in Syria have investigated some of these allegations and have found evidence that in some cases confirms and in others suggests that chemical weapons and/or toxic chemicals have been used in attacks by the Syrian regime and by the Islamic State. Syrian civilians, opposition fighters, and military personnel have been targeted in alleged attacks.[148]

Earlier U.N. and OPCW investigations had not been tasked with assigning responsibility for alleged attacks but with identifying whether chemical weapons were used. However, on August 7, 2015, the U.N. Security Council unanimously adopted Resolution 2235, which established a new OPCW-U.N. Joint Investigative Mechanism (JIM) tasked with identifying "to the greatest extent feasible" those responsible for or involved in chemical attacks identified by the OPCW fact finding mission.[149] In September 2015, the United Nations Security Council adopted the Secretary-General's proposal for the establishment of the OPCW-U.N. JIM, and the Secretary-General appointed Virginia Gamba of Argentina to head the independent three-member panel that leads the JIM.

While Resolution 2235 empowers the JIM to have access anywhere in Syria, the JIM's mission has been complicated by the security situation on the ground. The JIM initially investigated nine attacks alleged to have occurred between April 2014 and August 2015. Of these, three cases lacked sufficient evidence to draw conclusions, three cases require further investigation, and three cases were concluded. Eight of the cases involved chlorine-filled barrel bombs. The JIM

---

[145] Arms Control Association, "Timeline of Chemical Weapons Attacks in Syria: 2012-2017," fact sheet, 2017.

[146] Reports by U.N. Member States have been made via confidential correspondence, such as letters containing allegations described generally in the December 2013 final report of U.N. Mission to Investigate Allegations of the Use of Chemical Weapons in the Syrian Arab Republic (the U.N. Mission). See U.N. Mission, Final Report, December 12, 2013, pp. 2-6.

[147] The U.N. Mission to investigate Allegations of the Use of Chemical Weapons in the Syrian Arab Republic released its report on September 16, 2013, concluding that surface-to-surface rockets containing the chemical weapons nerve agent sarin were used in the Ghouta area of Damascus against civilians on a "relatively large scale." The 2013 U.N. investigative mission was not tasked with assigning culpability for the attacks.

[148] See U.N. Mission, *Final Report*, December 12, 2013; and OPCW Fact-Finding Mission (FFM) in Syria, Final Report, December 2015, attached to "Letter dated 27 January 2016 from the Secretary-General addressed to the President of the Security Council," S/2016/85, January 28, 2016.

[149] Resolution 2235 required that the U.N. Secretary-General, in coordination with the OPCW Director-General, submit within 20 days recommendations for its approval on the establishment of a Joint Investigative Mechanism "to identify to the greatest extent feasible individuals, entities, groups, or governments who were perpetrators, organisers [sic], sponsors or otherwise involved in the use of chemicals as weapons, including chlorine or any other toxic chemical, in the Syrian Arab Republic where the OPCW FFM determines or has determined that a specific incident in the Syrian Arab Republic involved or likely involved the use of chemicals as weapons, including chlorine or any other toxic chemical...."

submitted its third report on August 24, 2016, and its fourth report on October 21, 2016. The reports attributed four cases of chemical weapons use.[150] According to the report

- bombs with toxic chemicals (such as chlorine) were dropped in Talmenes in April 2014 by the Syrian Air Force;

- bombs with toxic chemicals (such as chlorine) were used in Qmenas in March 2015 by the Syrian Armed Forces;

- bombs with toxic chemicals (such as chlorine) were used in Sarmin in March 2015 by the Syrian Air Force; and,

- mortar shells filled with sulfur mustard were used by the Islamic State in Marea in August 2015.[151]

The Security Council extended the mandate of the JIM through 2017 despite initial objections by Russia, who argues for a wider regional mandate.[152] The JIM's mandate will remain limited to investigating alleged incidents of chemical weapons use in Syria, but will also include outreach to the UNSC's nonproliferation committee and neighboring states regarding non-state use of chemical weapons. The United States worked to extend the JIM, in order to "send a clear message that the use of chemical weapons will not be tolerated."[153]

The Syrian government continues to deny categorically that it has used chemical weapons or toxic chemicals, while accusing opposition forces of doing so and calling into question the methods and results of some investigations into alleged chemical attacks.[154] The Russian Federation supports the Syrian position. The U.N. representatives of the United States, France, and the United Kingdom continue to assert that the Syrian government has been conducting chemical attacks. An effort in February 2017 to pass a Security Council Resolution that would sanction Syria failed to get the votes of Russia or China.[155] The latest incidence of use on April 4

---

[150] Letter dated 24 August 2016 from the Leadership Panel of the Organization for the Prohibition of Chemical Weapons-United Nations Joint Investigative Mechanism addressed to the Secretary-General, S/2016/738; Letter dated 21 October 2016 from the Leadership Panel of the Organization for the Prohibition of Chemical Weapons-United Nations Joint Investigative Mechanism addressed to the Secretary-General, S/2016/888.

[151] The JIM report states that OPCW experts were able to identify that the sulfur mustard was produced by the Islamic State because of the way it was produced, which was different from Syrian government stocks. "The OPCW confirmed that the sulfur mustard from the Syrian Arab Republic did not contain impurities such as polysulphides, meaning that a different process was used by the Government. The OPCW also reported that the sulfur mustard used by ISIL in northern Iraq on several occasions in 2015 and 2016 was produced through the Levinstein process." Ibid, p. 97.

[152] "Syria: Renewal of the UN-OPCW Joint Investigative Mechanism," *What's In Blue*, November 17, 2016.

[153] Mark Toner, Deputy State Department Spokesman, "The Fourth Report of the Joint Investigative Mechanism," Press Statement, October 28, 2016.

[154] On August 7, the Permanent Representative of Syria to the United Nations Dr. Bashar Jaafari told the United Nations Security Council that, "the Syrian Government and the Syrian army have never used chemical weapons, and never will. Contrariwise, Syria's army and its civilians have been targeted with toxic chemicals and chemical weapons, including chlorine gas, by armed terrorist groups, such as *Daesh* [Arabic acronym for ISIL] and the Al-Nusra Front, in many parts of Syria… ." He accused unspecified investigation missions of having "based their work on false, fabricated statements made by parties well known to all. Those missions have carried out partial and biased investigations— outside Syria—without a modicum of coordination with the Syrian authorities." (U.N. Document S/PV.7501.) The U.N. and OPCW investigative missions have worked inside Syria with the permission of the Syrian government. In 2011, the U.N. Human Rights Council established an Independent International Commission of Inquiry on the Syrian Arab Republic that has reported extensively on the conflict, including on alleged chemical attacks. The Commission uses a "reasonable grounds to believe" standard of evidence and relies on first-hand accounts from Syrians now in neighboring countries, remote interviews, and other publicly available information.

[155] "Syria Draft Resolution Imposing Sanctions Regarding the Use and Production of Chemical Weapons," *What's In Blue*, February 25, 2017.

has elevated these issues again to the U.N. Security Council where Russia defends the Syrian stance. The United States, United Kingdom, and France proposed a U.N. Security Council Resolution in support of a U.N. investigation into who was responsible for the April 4 attack, but this resolution was vetoed by Russia. Nevertheless, the U.N. and OPCW mechanisms already in place from past Security Council resolutions, the Fact Finding Mission (FFM) and the Joint Investigative Mechanism (JIM), have begun an investigation into the April 4 attack.

Additional press reports have reported on possible use of mustard gas in Syria and Iraq by IS fighters.[156] The OPCW's chief has said that the Islamic State has produced and used sulfur mustard in northern Iraq and Syria.[157] U.S. forces struck Islamic State sites in Iraq believed to be associated with chemical weapons production in September 2016, and a multilateral effort removed chemical weapons precursors from Libya in August 2016 after Islamic State affiliate forces threatened the area where the materials had been stored in that country. The Pentagon has said that U.S. troops fighting in Iraq are expected to continue to face weaponized mustard gas attacks by the Islamic State.[158] As recently as April 15, press reports said that the Islamic State had used chemical weapons against Iraqi forces in Mosul.[159]

Outlook

Following the April chemical weapons attack, President Trump and his Administration have expressed increased concern about Syrian President Bashar al Asad and skepticism regarding the legitimacy of his continued rule. Speaking on April 7, U.S. Permanent Representative to the United Nations Ambassador Nikki Haley spoke of "a new phase" and "a drive toward a political solution," following Secretary of State Tillerson's outline of U.S. goals for Syria on April 6.[160] That outline prioritizes action against the Islamic State in pursuit of a political solution "that ultimately, in our view, will lead to a resolution of Bashar al Asad's departure."[161]

Asad and Russia continue to reject calls for what they describe as Western-led regime change in Syria, and argue that counterterrorism cooperation with the Syrian government against its adversaries should precede further discussion of transition arrangements. Efforts to forcefully compel Asad's departure or empower opposition groups to depose Asad may risk direct confrontation with Russian military forces, with potentially broad implications beyond Syria. At the same time, the risk remains that any perceived U.S. acquiescence to or cooperation with Russia's intervention on Asad's behalf risks alienating anti-Asad forces and their regional backers, as well as providing Russia with an opportunity to consolidate a new, active role for itself in regional security arrangements.

Over the longer term, Syria's diversity and the interplay of its conflict and regional sectarian rivalries raise the prospect of continued violence even in the wake of the type of "managed

---

[156] "U.S. Tests Show Mustard Gas Traces in Islamic State Attack," *The Washington Post,* August 21, 2015.

[157] Slovenia Press Agency, "IS Likely Used Chemical Weapons in Syria, Iraq; Could Use Them Elsewhere, OPCW Head Says," May 11, 2016.

[158] "U.S.: Shell That Hit Iraqi Base Contained Sulfur-Mustard Agent," *Associated Press,* September 22, 2016; "U.S. Troops Brace for More Mustard Attacks," *Military Times,* September 27, 2016.

[159] "ISIS Militants Launch Multiple Chemical Weapons Attacks on Iraqi Troops," *Newsweek,* April 17, 2017; "Chemical Attacks and Narrow Streets Complicate Fight for Mosul's Old City, "*Al-Monitor,* April 2017; "The Islamic State threatens more chemical attacks in Mosul after loss of senior ISIS commander," *SOFREP News,* April 20, 2017.

[160] U.S. Permanent Representative to the United Nations Ambassador Nikki Haley, Remarks at a U.N. Security Council Meeting on the Situation in Syria, April 7, 2017.

[161] Secretary of State Rex Tillerson, Remarks with National Security Advisor H.R. McMaster, April 6, 2017.

transition" that has at times been identified as a U.S. policy goal. The presence and power in Syria of armed groups directly opposed to the governance models promoted by many Syrians and the United States suggests that the conflict could persist after any negotiated settlement seeking to replace the current Asad-led government with a government of national unity or other inclusive formulation. Political opposition coalitions active internationally appear to lack grassroots support and, because of their lack of material control over the most powerful armed groups, they appear to lack the ability to guarantee security commitments that might presumably be part of a negotiated settlement. Some analysts doubt the Asad government could survive a partial transition and suggest state collapse could accompany efforts to replace it whether by negotiation or by force. Even under relatively favorable circumstances, state weakness may allow extremist and terrorist groups to operate from Syria for years to come.

Observers, U.S. officials, and Members of Congress continue to differ over which incentives and disincentives may prove most effective in influencing combatants and their supporters. Still less defined are the long-term commitments that the United States and others may be willing to make to achieve an inclusive political transition acceptable to Syrians; protect civilians; defend U.S. partners; promote accountability and reconciliation; or contribute to the rebuilding of a country destroyed by years of brutal war.

Author Contact Information

Carla E. Humud, Coordinator
Analyst in Middle Eastern Affairs
chumud@crs.loc.gov, 7-7314

Christopher M. Blanchard
Specialist in Middle Eastern Affairs
cblanchard@crs.loc.gov, 7-0428

Mary Beth D. Nikitin
Specialist in Nonproliferation
mnikitin@crs.loc.gov, 7-7745